Studies in
Writing & Rhetoric

IN 1980, THE CONFERENCE ON COLLEGE COMPOSITION AND COM-
munication perceived a need for providing publishing opportunities
for monographs that were too lengthy for publication in its journal
and too short for the typical publication of scholarly books by The
National Council of Teachers of English. A series called Studies in
Writing and Rhetoric was conceived, and a Publication Committee
established.

Monographs to be considered for publication may be speculative,
theoretical, historical, or analytical studies; research reports; or
other works contributing to a better understanding of writing, including interdisciplinary studies or studies in disciplines related to
composing. The SWR series will exclude textbooks, unrevised dis-
sertations, book-length manuscripts, course syllabi, lesson plans,
and collections of previously published material.

Any teacher-writer interested in submitting a work for publication in this series should send either a prospectus and sample manuscript or a full manuscript to the NCTE Coordinator of Professional
Publications, 1111 Kenyon Road, Urbana, IL 61801. Accompanied
by sample manuscript, a prospectus should contain a rationale, a
definition of readership within the CCCC constituency, comparison
with related publications, an annotated table of contents, an estimate of length in double-spaced 8½ × 11 sheets, and the date by
which full manuscript can be expected. Manuscripts should be in
the range of 100 to 170 typed manuscript pages.

The works that have been published in this series serve as models
for future SWR monographs.

NCTE Coordinator of Professional Publications

Writing Groups
History, Theory, and Implications

Anne Ruggles Gere

WITH A FOREWORD BY JERRIE COBB SCOTT

Published for the Conference on College
Composition and Communication

SOUTHERN ILLINOIS UNIVERSITY PRESS
Carbondale and Edwardsville

Production of works in this series has been partly funded by the Conference on College Composition and Communication of the National Council of Teachers of English.

Printed in the United States of America
Designed by Design for Publishing, Inc., Bob Nance
Edited by Genevieve Gwynne
Production supervised by Natalia Nadraga

90 89 88 87   4 3 2 1

Library of Congress Cataloging-in-Publication Data

Gere, Anne Ruggles, 1944–
  Writing groups.

  (Studies in writing & rhetoric)
  Bibliography: p.
  1. English language—Rhetoric—Study and teaching (Higher) 2. Group work in education.
I. Title. II. Series.
PE1404.G44   1987   808'.042'07   86-26137
ISBN 0-8093-1354-5

For Budge

Contents

Foreword

Jerrie Cobb Scott

OF LATE WE HEAR AND READ A LOT ABOUT THE SUCCESS OF
writing groups in composition classes—how well-managed writing
groups benefit the teacher, or how the sharing among students and
between teacher and students benefits students. Focusing on the
use of writing groups as a teaching method, much of the recent
literature is pragmatic in its orientation. But as Anne Gere points
out, pragmatism does not tell the whole story. Gere relates a fuller
story about writing groups—how they emerged, why they serve the
needs of the writer, and what their historical development and theoretical underpinnings mean in terms of defining writing and preparing students to participate in the literate community of educated
people. Accordingly, *Writing Groups: History, Theory, and Implications* emphasizes the broader significance of writing groups.

The central theme of this book is that "writing groups represent a
specific instance of writing's social dimension." This theme is the tie
that binds history to theory to implications about what it means to
write. Thus, Gere adds to the continuing dialogue on writing groups
an understanding of the social dimension of writing. Tracing the history of writing groups in this country from the Colonial period to
the present, Gere gives the reader a sense of the complex social
forces that led to the formation of writing groups both within and
outside academic settings. Sexism, for example, was directly responsible for the formation of separate men's and women's mutual
improvement societies, often the progenitors of early writing
groups; one wonders how this separation influenced both the social

interaction among participants and the meaning they constructed. Her treatment of writing groups not only broadens our understanding of their historical significance, but it also provides "tangible evidence that writing involves human interaction as well as solitary performance."

Since composition theory and pedagogy have derived largely from the epistemological assumptions of nineteenth-century rhetoric, it is not surprising that most discussions of writing groups focus on the intellectual development of the solitary writer. Central to writing groups, though, is the interaction among participants, obviously an important aspect of the social dimension of writing. Theories of writing as a social act do exist, but they have not previously been applied to writing groups. By examining theories of collaboration, audience, language development, and evaluation, Gere "makes explicit some of the underlying assumptions of writing groups' procedures and results." The reader comes to see that the aesthetic and epistemological concern with the author must be broadened to include the notion of the writer as a social actor, engaged with others in the creation of meaning.

For Gere, becoming literate means "joining a specific community through understanding the issues it considers important and developing the capacity to participate in conversations about those issues." This definition of literacy is ideological rather than technical, and Gere argues from it that "one of the tasks facing every educator, and particularly every composition instructor, is that of initiating students in the language of the educated world." And writing groups offer one way that teachers can meet the demands of that task. From a broader perspective, though, socially based views of writing, like socially based views of literacy, can lead to new ways of looking at and defining writing. Toward this end, Gere's examination of the social dimension of writing groups makes a significant contribution.

Writing Groups establishes a conceptual framework for rethinking what it means to write, a framework for broadening our definitions of writing to include the social dimension. Broader definitions need not, indeed should not, exclude the individual dimension of writing. As Gere puts it, "the authority of individual creation can coexist with the authority of consensus." Gere's intent is not to create oppositions, but "to transform dichotomy into dialogue." The newly acquired status of writing groups, the cross-disciplinary inquiries into socially defined views of knowledge, the current theoretical interest in defining, describing, and explaining the writing process—all these combine to make this a very timely book. It challenges the reader, teacher, theorist, and writer to participate in the dialogue, to help discover what it means to write, and more specifically, what it means to write both solitarily and collaboratively.

Acknowledgments

ONE WHO WRITES ABOUT THE SOCIAL DIMENSION OF COMPOSING cannot ignore the many interactions that helped shape language. The genesis of this book lies in my own participation in writing groups, a participation that began as I worked with teachers in the Puget Sound Writing Program. Ralph Stevens, along with Roger Whitlock and Carolyn Woodward, initiated me into a writing group in the summer of 1979, and from that time forward I have regularly shared my work-in-progress with a small group of writers. Marcia Barton, John Campbell, Linda Clifton, Mary Kollar, Tom Roesler, Margaret Scarborough, Charles Schuster, Sandra Silberstein, Susan Starbuck, Linda Sullivan, Kate Vangen, and Barbara Warnick have, in the intervening years, joined me in an ongoing conversation about writing.

Puget Sound Writing Program teachers who initiated writing groups in their own classes helped me see the need to learn more about these groups. A grant from the National Institute of Education made systematic investigation possible, and Catherine Butler, Lori Eichelberg, Lynn Howgate, Beverly Leonard, and Susan Sailer graciously opened their classrooms to observers with tape recorders. Collaborating on subsequent articles with Robert Abbott and Ralph Stevens enriched my understanding of what the classroom study had produced and at the same time highlighted its limitations.

Professional leave from the University of Washington gave me time to correct these limitations by looking at writing groups more completely. As I worked on this book, conversations with Karen Blair, Kenneth Bruffee, Robert Connors, Peter Elbow, James Gray, Kenneth Kantor, Barry Kroll, Richard Lloyd-Jones, Donald Murray, Thomas Newkirk, Martin Nystrand, Jodie Reed, David Russell,

Lewis Saum, Donald Stewart, and Barbara Tomlinson helped me understand writing groups more fully. Correspondence with Ken Macrorie, James Moffett, and Stephen Wilbers likewise aided my thinking. Kenneth Bruffee, Budge Gere, William Irmscher, Donald Murray, Eugene Smith, and John Trimbur, along with members of the Studies in Writing and Rhetoric selection committee, made many helpful suggestions for revision. Rob Weller of the University of Washington's Humanities and Arts Computing Center eased the technical dimensions of these revisions, and Dan Gunter of the SIU Press guided the editorial process thoughtfully and skillfully.

In this, as in all my writing, my family provided the right mixture of indulgence, encouragement, humor, and pressure. Cindy and Sam tolerated my long sessions with the computer but insisted that I keep up with their regular routines and join them for bike rides and skiing. Budge picked up extra household duties when I faced deadlines and offered support when I faltered but reminded me to keep work balanced with love.

Writing Groups

Introduction

WRITING GROUPS, THE PARTNER METHOD, HELPING CIRCLES, collaborative writing, response groups, team writing, writing laboratories, teacherless writing classes, group inquiry technique, the round table, class criticism, editing sessions, writing teams, workshops, peer tutoring, the socialized method, mutual improvement sessions, intensive peer review—the phenomenon has nearly as many names as people who employ it. The name, of course, matters less than what it describes, which is writers responding to one another's work. Writing groups, as I choose to call them, operate both within and outside schools. Specifics, like the names, vary. Groups range in size from three to more than forty. When writing groups meet in classroom, some instructors structure tasks and provide explicit direction, while others avoid interfering with student commentary. Some groups exchange written drafts and receive verbal or written comments, while some read aloud and receive oral response. Some shift the procedure to suit the material (reading long essays or poems and listening to shorter prose selections, for example). Groups observe differing codes for response. Some intervene directly in members' writing—helping generate ideas or telling the writer what to do next—while others restrict responses to what has already been written.

This ambiguity of terminology and procedure reflects the larger ambiguity facing the field of composition studies. Fretted as it is by the pressure of working with students who cannot write the clear and effective prose that will satisfy the stringent but evanescent standards imposed by other instructors, by future employers, and by the larger society, composition studies has frequently skirted theory in favor of practice. Operating without a coherent theory and frequently with little information about what their peers do, individual instructors have created their own versions of "works good." Frequently these instructors have gone on to justify their practice with publication, sometimes prefacing publication with empirical investigation. But theoretical support for and examination of what works in the classroom has developed much more slowly, as composition studies has begun to transform itself from a field where graduate education consists of the "informal curriculum" of texts designed for freshman writing classes into one that has its own scholarly tradition.

Creating this scholarly tradition means moving from exigency to exegesis, from responding to the needs of the moment to thinking about what that response means. This study contributes to that tradition by considering writing groups in terms that extend beyond the practical. There is no shortage of publications on methodological dimensions of writing groups. Hundreds of articles and scores of books detail procedures by which writers meet and respond to one another's writing. Instructors interested in using writing groups in their classes or individuals seeking to establish their own groups can find, scattered throughout the literature, explanations of when and how to form groups, strategies for training group participants, ways to establish criteria for judging writing, variations on group procedures, descriptions of types of groups, lists of advantages inherent in using groups, and evidence of the effectiveness of writing groups in improving writing.

Although valuable for classroom implementation, a methodological perspective helps create the impression that writing groups constitute one more approach, one more in a series of remedies for beleaguered instructors. As such they receive the isolated treatment frequently given "mere pedagogy." Even authors who ask interesting questions about, say, the effects of writing groups on intellectual development or their contribution to positive attitudes about writing do so in isolation from one another.

One consequence of this isolation appears in the number of articles that describe writing groups as "novel" or "innovative." A quick survey of titles listed in part 1 of the Bibliography demonstrates how many times writing groups have been "discovered." This recurring assertion of the novelty of writing groups not only impoverishes the quality of discussion about them but also emphasizes their differences rather than their similarities. Each author who employs the terminology of innovation contributes to an artificial separation of one writing group from another: artificial because regardless of their multiple names and various procedures, writing groups of all sizes share a number of common features. In temporal terms, all writing groups provide response with an immediacy impossible in teachers' marginalia or reviewers' evaluations. Whether they receive comments from three individuals or a classroom full of people, writing group participants do not have to wait days or months to learn what others think of their work. In physical terms, writing groups reduce the distance between writer and reader. Even when responses take written form, authors operate in close proximity to an audience, enjoying opportunities to observe the effects of their work or to ask questions.

Perhaps the most significant commonality among writing groups appears in what they contribute to our understanding of what it means to write. Specifically, writing groups highlight the social dimension of writing. They provide tangible evidence that writing involves human interaction as well as solitary inscription. Highlighting the social dimension enlarges our view of writing because composition studies has, until recently, conceptualized writing as a solo performance. A variety of forces, ranging from aspects of intellectual history to social institutions such as copyright law, have contributed to the dominance of a solo-performer view of writing.

Untangling the complexities of institutions and intellect that have led composition studies to prize individual effort over social interaction in writing extends beyond the scope of this book. A specific instance of writing's social dimension does appear, however, in writing groups. An examination of writing groups is timely because of the new status they have attained in recent years. Although they have existed in various forms for more than two hundred years, institutionalization has marked writing groups in the past decade as increasing numbers of instructors made them a regular part of the curriculum. The significant increases in the volume of publication (see part 1 of the Bibliography) on writing groups provides one indication of recent institutionalization. This examination is timely also because the intellectual ground supporting the solo performer is shifting. A variety of disciplines are moving toward a socially defined view of knowledge, and this transition suggests a need to expand the concept of writing beyond the solo performer.

This book, then, explores the social dimension of writing through considering several aspects of writing groups. In so doing it attempts to enlarge upon the methodological emphasis common in discussions of writing groups. Logistical considerations of how to establish, maintain, and evaluate writing groups therefore play a minor role, appearing only in chapter 5 and in the annotated listing of articles in the Bibliography.

In insisting upon the commonality conferred by the social dimension of writing, this book does not ignore important differences among writing groups. These differences center on the origins of authority. Both historically and in the present, writing groups convene in two ways—voluntarily and involuntarily. When groups form voluntarily, authority originates in individual members who choose, for reasons of friendship, solidarity, respect, or need, to give, temporarily at least, authority over their writing to others. These autonomous groups stand in contrast to groups convened involuntarily—usually in classrooms—where authority originates outside the individual members. Here it is the teacher or other individual charged with directing activities who has the authority to initiate group work. Although classroom groups may achieve a semi-autonomous status, the institutional origins of authority prevent them from becoming completely autonomous. And frequently they remain entirely nonautonomous.

Three dimensions—history, theory, and implications—shape this book. The historical dimension addresses the isolation exemplified by recurring articles that describe writing groups as "new" or "experimental" or "just discovered" at the same time that it supplies another piece of the past for composition studies. In exploring the complex forces that led to today's writing groups, this historical section demonstrates that writing groups are both old and new. Chapter 1 traces classroom writing groups to undergraduate literary societies active between the colonial period and the middle of the nineteenth century, showing how academic institutions incorporated these groups into the curriculum. It also considers the influence of four late-nineteenth-century educational reform movements upon classroom writing groups at all levels of education, and it illustrates how these four movements contribute to the thinking of contemporary writing group advocates such as James Moffett, Donald Murray, Ken Macrorie, and Ken Bruffee. Self-sponsored writing groups, those that stand outside educational institutions, receive consideration in chapter 2. In following the progression from colonial clubs to young men's associations to the Lyceum and Chautauqua movements to women's clubs to contemporary groups that follow Peter Elbow's advise to "write without teachers," this chapter demonstrates that writers who gathered to critique one another's work two hundred years ago were guided by many of the same impulses that guide members of today's writing groups.

The theoretical section of this book makes explicit some of the assumptions underlying writing group procedures and results. It provides a map of the territory, indicating boundaries between writing groups and related domains and illustrating why some courses open new territories and others lead into thickets. Chapter 3 juxtaposes the theory of collaboration to the traditional concept of "author," calling attention to the political and economic factors that joined with intellectual forces to shape the latter. After discussing how the concept of author has dominated much of composition studies, this chapter proposes the alternative of a social view of writing and of knowledge, one that reduces alienation through collaboration. The contrast between seeing language as a conduit or conveyer of thought and seeing language as the medium in which ideas are developed is explored in chapter 4. Piaget's view of the asocial genesis of language represents one pole while Vygotsky's concept of the social origins of language represents the other, and this chapter demonstrates the limitations imposed by restricting thought about writing to Piaget's asocial model. Implicit in both chapters in this section is the assumption that traditional Cartesian epistemology undercuts the theoretical bases upon which writing groups operate, that seeing knowledge as socially constructed offers a more congenial alternative.

The final section of this book considers the implications of writing groups in both practical and theoretical terms. Leaving specific methodological directives to others, chapter 5 examines elements of preparation, commitment, clarity and appropriateness of task, and evaluation common to effective writing groups. In distinguishing between autonomous self-sponsored groups and the semi-autonomous or nonautonomous groups that emerge in classrooms, it illustrates the centrality of considering issues of authority in these groups. Starting from the assertion that writing groups finally concern themselves with literacy, chapter 6 considers two perspectives on literacy—the skills/technology view and the ideological view. Arguing that becoming literate means joining a community, this chapter asserts that the ideological view is consonant with writing groups because both portray writing in social terms.

In advancing the case for a social dimension in writing, this book does not negate the concept of the individual author. Writing has, of course its solitary side, and all writers must at some time be solo performers. But this book speaks to a more comprehensive definition of writing, one that incorporates individual *and* social dimensions. It assumes that the authority of individual creation can coexist with the authority of consensus.

Two scientific principles suggest a way to incorporate the concept of writer as solo performer with the concept of writer as social participant. The principle of indeterminacy explains that the same elements can behave in two different ways depending upon their environment. Light, for example, behaves like particles at some times and like waves at others. Transposing this principle to composition helps us acknowledge that writers do not possess intrinsic qualities that remain the same under all conditions. Sometimes they operate as solo performers, isolating themselves in order to inscribe words on blank pages, and at other times they interact with their peers to share, discuss, and receive suggestions on their work. The principle of complementarity recognizes that two opposing theories can operate simultaneously in different spheres as do, say, Newtonian physics and quantum theory. When applied to composition studies, this principle enables us to accept the idea that the social dimension of writing applies in some cases while the individual dimension dominates in others. In considering the history, theory, and implications of writing groups, this book contributes to the rapprochement between writer as solo performer and writer as social actor. It helps transform dichotomy into dialogue.

Part 1

History

1

Writing Groups
in Academic Institutions

ASK MOST COMPOSITION INSTRUCTORS ABOUT THE ORIGINS OF
writing groups, and you will hear responses such as, "They started
in the sixties, when student-centered learning was so popular," or,
"Peter Elbow developed them, or was it Ken Macrorie? No, maybe
it was Donald Murray." They may credit a particular individual or a
specific period in history, but these instructors will identify writing
groups as recent developments. For evidence they will point to current publications, conferences, or their own recent practice of asking groups of students to critique one another's writing.

A smaller number of instructors will claim that writing groups have
existed as long as writers have shared their work with peers and received commentary on it. They will cite groups of famous authors
who congregated in Paris or New York or the Bloomsbury district
of London. Or they will mention long-standing writers' workshops
and/or their own experiences with response groups. Both are right:
Writing groups are new *and* old. They also appear in various forms
and sizes, ranging from a large (from twenty to thirty) number of
people who offer a formal critique after an entire paper has been
read aloud, to a group of three to five individuals who respond informally to shorter selections. In all their manifestations, however,
writing groups conceive of writing in social terms.

This chapter and the next trace writing group history back to the
early days of the United States. In so doing, they validate the double
truth of these groups' novelty and longevity. New writing groups
form continually as interest in them burgeons, but other groups can

trace their ancestry back to the early part of this century. Writing groups did not spring from a single source; rather, they emerged from several institutions and intellectual traditions. Among them are the college literary societies that began forming during this country's colonial period.

Most literary societies emerged as a forum in which students debated public issues, but "assigning and criticizing compositions" soon numbered among their functions (Potter 70). The students who initiated these groups took an active interest in improving their writing skills. Literary societies were founded between the first part of the eighteenth century and the late nineteenth century at various colleges and universities in this country. One of the earliest such groups, The Spy Club, was organized at Harvard in 1719, and other groups followed close behind. Philomausarian was founded in 1728, The Speaking Club in 1770, and Hasty Pudding in 1795. Students at other colleges of the colonial period likewise established literary societies. Criterion, a student society at Yale, existed before 1750. The Flat Hat Club was established at the College of William and Mary in 1750 and included Thomas Jefferson among its members. The American Revolution occasioned many debates, and literary societies allowed students to take "the negative and the affirmative." One meeting of Harvard's Speaking Club in the early 1780s was, for example, devoted to the topic of "the pernicious habit of drinking tea" (Thwing 375).

This concern with political issues remained constant for literary societies in succeeding years. The Zelosophic Society, founded at the University of Pennsylvania in 1892, grew out of student concern with President Andrew Jackson's removal of officials from the previous administration. Students debated whether experience in office or opportunities for new leaders should be the guiding principle of presidential appointments. In the process of debating they formed Zelo, where they discussed "not only the removal question, but, as time went on, other problems and questions as well" (Sochatoff 29). The Literary Adelphi Society, founded in 1857 at the University of Michigan, included in its business meetings discussions of topics such as the statehood of Kansas (1860), U.S. intervention in Cuba's battle for independence (1896), and the role of the United States in the Philippines (1907).

Although political issues were central, they provided only one impetus for forming literary societies. Another was social need. For students of the eighteenth century, social life lacked richness and variety. Coeducational activites, athletics, cultural resources, cosmopolitan communities surrounding colleges, and many other diversions taken for granted by today's students were not available. Weekly literary society meetings provided nineteenth-century students a welcome social outlet. As the stated purpose of Literary Adelphi ("to foster a sense of personal responsibility for acquiring something of intellectual culture") indicates, literary societies were not founded explicitly for social reasons even though they often filled that function. In this, literary societies were distinctly different from the fraternities or secret societies that developed during the middle of the nineteenth century. Fraternities lacked the intellectual center common to literary societies. In fact, some commentators blame fraternities for the demise of literary societies (Aubry; Potter 93).

Faculty support and participation provided a major source of intellectual vitality in literary societies, and faculty members took an active role in their formation and continuation. It was a faculty member who encouraged students at the University of Pennsylvania to form the Zelosophic Society, and faculty names appeared on the membership rolls of many societies across the country. On some occasions faculty became too active, leading to student complaints. Records of the University of Michigan's Quadrangle Club, for example, include "To the LYFMOQS," a selection complaining about the dominance of the "Loquacious Younger Faculty Members of Quadrangle Society."

Despite such problems, literary societies benefited from faculty members (even the disgruntled author of "To the LYFMOQS" acknowledges the value of faculty participation) because these instructors fostered intellectual growth among members. A tangible sign of this growth appeared in the libraries established by literary societies. During the nineteenth century college libraries were frequently off limits to many students. One poignant first-person account describes an undergraduate watching privileged upperclassmen entering the stacks of the library. The author fantasizes about the day when he will join the select group and considers the appropriate bearing to assume when he steps across the forbidden threshold (Quadrangle). When available to students, libraries were often sad collections of the "chance aggregations of the gifts of charity" (Lyle 492) and did not have systematic acquisition procedures or sufficient funds to purchase contemporary literature. Consequently, most literary societies established their own libraries.

As much as current events, faculty participation, and libraries contributed to intellectual stimulation, they took second place to literary exercises in most societies. These orations, compositions, forensic debates, disputations, humorous dialogues, essays, or music/ drama productions constituted societies' central activity. Literary exercises gave members a reason to gather week after week in their meeting rooms. From their earliest days, many literary societies critiqued their own exercises. Linonia, the society founded at Yale in 1753, began with an array of exercises, and in 1769 criticism of the evening's performance was added to the program. Criticism extended to written as well as oral language, and responding to one another's writing was part of the regular routine of most societies through the middle of the nineteenth century. When they began presenting and receiving criticism on their work, students in literary societies inaugurated what we would call writing groups.

Some societies, reflecting the seriousness with which they viewed criticism of speech and writing in their meetings, created the office of critic. This person led critical responses to an evening's exercises. George Cutting, describing Amherst College's societies of the early ninetenth century, writes: "The critic's department in those early days had a significance which meant something. In the Athenian Society he had to criticise all compositions before they could be read before the society" (18). Many critics of the latter part of the nineteenth century likewise took their duties seriously. H. D. Dunning, a newly elected critic, included these words of assurance in his acceptance letter to Michigan's Alpha Nu Society in 1852:

> Having had the benefits and horrors of criticism inflicted upon myself at divers times and in sundry manners, I have learned to sympathize with its victim, and I feel a real pain when I see him switching and twisting under its tortures. I shall, therefore, give no unnecessary slashes, and distribute them impartially. Many seem to form the idea that a critic must be a kind of bull dog snorter, smacking his sharp incisors into the nervous legs of those who may be so unfortunate as to come within the

limits of his doggy dominance, and occasionally giving some poor fellow a severe laceration for his daring presumption.

There may be, perhaps there are some who thus give vent to their lamentable envy, and are ever "showing their teeth" by way of snap, yet others soon learn that they are more to be despised than dreaded and seldom notice, or shake a stick at them. Grumbling and censoriousny [sic] is not the sphere of cricitism. It transcends all low, mean considerations and can praise, when consistent, as well as censure. It is indeed an honorable and useful art, when properly conducted. As we are generally blind to a degree to our own faults, a hint, or a suggestion from another relative to them, may cause us to see and abandon defects and errors of which we might long have remained in ignorance.

Despite its slightly archaic language, this excerpt provides insights into the nature of criticism in Dunning's Alpha Nu Literary Society, criticism similar to that in any writing group. Its reassuring tone, eschewing censure and grumbling, acknowledges that criticism in any writing group, whether by elected officers or by all members, does not proceed autocratically. Rather it depends upon the willingness of members to lend, temporarily at least, authority to one another's responses. Dunning's observation about writers' blindness to their own faults implies a recognition of both rhetorical and intellectual dimensions of writing. In rhetorical terms, the critic's observations enhance writers' audience awareness, helping them to see their work from the perspective of others. At the same time intellectual growth results from enhanced self-critical abilities fostered by recognizing one's own "defects and errors."

Useful as they were, literary societies underwent major changes in the late nineteenth century, and most either took new form or disbanded in response to new institutions on campus. The emergence of fraternities contributed, as was noted earlier, to the disappearance of literary societies. But academic as well as social forces usurped literary society functions. During the second half of the nineteenth century, libraries received more funding and became systematic in acquisition, rendering the societies' libraries unnecessary (Thwing 409–17). Another kind of appropriation occurred as college curricula absorbed work formerly carried out by societies. Because they adapted new forms quickly and were closer to the undergraduate pulse than college administrators or faculties, literary societies had always supplied college curricula with some innovations. Forensic debate, for example, had been featured in literary societies before it appeared in college classes. But a much more thoroughgoing appropriation occurred as English departments began to appear on college campuses during the last three decades of the nineteenth century. These new departments absorbed most of the literary discussion and writing instruction formerly carried out in literary societies: robbed of this central function, societies began to change or die.

Change was, of course, not new for literary societies; they continually took different forms. For example, Yale's Criterion (date unknown) gave way to Linonia (1753), which in turn spawned Brothers in Unity (1768) and Calliope (1819) (Coe). Amherst's Alexandrian and Athenian gave rise to Social Union, and later all three disappeared to make way for Academia and Eclectic (Cutting 36–37). Accordingly, while academic appropriation caused some societies to disband, it led others to metamorphose. When English composition began to enter college curricula in the late nineteenth century, it rarely included the peer critique central to literary societies, so groups that survived (or were formed) during that period concentrated on writing-group functions.

In 1895, the Knights of English Learning, "a voluntary society auxiliary to the [English] department" at the University of Minnesota, emphasized "the hearing and discussion of the results of special work by students" (MacLean 157–58). During the same period, students at the University of Illinois were allowed to submit in their required rhetoric and theme-writing classes compositions produced for "the various college societies" (Dodge 73), and this extracurricular writing was taken as seriously as any produced in a class. David Frankenburger, writing about late-nineteenth-century English instruction at the University of Wisconsin, explains the importance of the literary societies on his campus: "They form a great practice department in English composition and elocution. The work is so certain, and so uniform in quality, that it may be looked upon as part, and not an unimportant part either, of the students' training" (138).

Members of these groups, who wanted to learn and practice the craft of writing, followed procedures similar to those of today's writing groups. Describing the methods of University of Iowa clubs such as Tabard (1891–96), Polygon (1893–1913), and Ivy Lane (1894–1923), Stephen Wilbers writes: "Their purpose was to improve the participants' skills as writers by allowing each member to have a turn reading his or her original work, after which the groups would respond with suggestions and literary criticism" (20). This procedure emulated the critique sessions of literary societies and enabled students to help one another improve their writing.

Literary societies and/or writers' clubs provided a model for yet another appropriation by college curricula. As Wilbers notes, "While there was nothing particularly unique about this approach (writers have always asked friends and colleagues for feedback), the practice formalized by these clubs provided a format that could be incorporated into the classroom" (20). And incorporated it was. At Iowa, for instance, "the method [of peer response] (later to be called the 'workshop' approach) was adopted by the University when it offered its first course in creative writing entitled 'Verse-making Class,' in the spring of 1897" (Wilbers 20). Many colleges and universities followed this pattern of adapting literary society/writers' club activities to fiction and poetry classes. Another form of appropriation occurred with the formation of programs such as the Bread Loaf Writers' Conference. In 1926, Paul Moody, President of Middlebury College, joined Robert Frost and John Farrar, then editor of *Bookman*, to create the conference with the stated purpose of providing writers a place "to show their work-in-progress to a responsive group who could comment on it with authority" (Abel 1). According to the present director, writing groups have always been part of Bread Loaf. The second week is "devoted to the reading of student manuscripts before all of the Conference. An instructor reads from a manuscript and then invites peer response" (Cubeta).

This progression from literary society to writers' club to classroom workshop outlines the evolution to writing groups in college classes, but frequently these groups appeared only in creative writing classes. The long-standing division between "creative" writing and the other kind bred suspicion between representatives of the two. Donald Murray's description of his own experience illustrates: "Even after *A Writer Teaches Writing* came out in 1968, I was not allowed to be on the Freshman English Committee because I was a writer. . . . I was invited to become chairperson of Freshman English in 1972, most likely by default, and there was great concern in the department about that" (letter). Still, many college instructors brought writing groups into "regular" composition courses. John Genung, identified by Albert Kitzhaber as one of the "Big Four" of the nineteenth century who shaped writing instruction in this country, described composition classes at Amherst College as carrying out "laboratory work." According to Genung, instructors ran workshops that included, among other things, "the setting up in type of many of the students' written productions, and the reading and criticism of them in proof" (113). A student's recollection of classes taught by University of Michigan professor Fred Newton Scott, another of the "Big Four," includes Scott's practice of asking students to read their work aloud for class response (Smith 279).

The 1895 English program at Yale described a senior composition class this way: "A weekly class-room exercise will be occupied with discussion and criticism of speciman themes" (Cook 33). A description of the same period from the University of Pennsylvania asserts that "every composition is read,—occasionally before the class or a section of it" (Schelling 131). In 1895, instructors at Johns Hopkins University taught a course in rhetoric and English composition that included this procedure with papers: "they are read and criticised from week to week in the presence of the class" (James Bright 152). In 1901 students at MIT took a composition course in which 50 percent of their grade depended upon their critiques of one another's papers (Valentine). In 1914 Middlebury College introduced a "laboratory" course in which students criticized one another's writing (Cady 76). This laboratory may have paved the way for The Bread Loaf Writers Conference, and if it did, it reversed the usual pattern of moving writing groups from creative to expository writing classes.

Few commentators include information about the substance of student critiques, but Valentine, in his description of the 1901 course at MIT, reproduces a number of student papers complete with peer comments. These comments, to the extent that they can be regarded as typical, show that student writing groups of that period dealt with local as well as global aspects of writing. For example, in response to the sentence "after doing this we had a pretty substantial framework for our little cabin," the student comment reads "omit pretty" (470). Frequently students request clarification. In response to a description of recovering by-products in a blast furnace, a student writes, "I should like to know how the gases pass from one pipe to another; do they pass up one pipe and then down the next?" (475). Summative comments at the end of papers deal with more global issues such as focus and audience awareness. Examples include: "In discussing what good times you had at the little camp and in telling why you went there you forgot your subject was on building a camp not what you did there" (471) and (in response to a paper on learning to play golf) "I hardly think a beginner would succeed if he followed your instructions in some cases. You have left out some very important parts on how to distribute the strength of the stroke, which if not made clear to the novice, will cause him much trouble" (473).

Writing groups also insinuated themselves into secondary school classrooms. From 1880 forward, articles describing and/or recommending writing groups appeared in publications for high school teachers (see the Bibliography). A century ago, as now, advantages attributed to writing groups included increasing student motivation toward writing, and particularly toward revising (Cooper; Lord); developing greater audience awareness (Buck; Thurber; Watt); fostering critical capacities and intellectual precision (Noyes; Tressler); and creating a positive classroom atmosphere along with enhancing the self-image of individual students (Leonard "Two Types"; Francis Walker; Ziegler). And, then as now, teachers struggling with large student loads turned to writing groups to lighten the burden. In an 1870 secondary school text, for example, Richard Parker suggested that teachers faced with large composition classes might ask students to critique one another's writing (370).

The attention researchers gave writing groups during the early decades of this century evinces the seriousness attached to them. In 1919, for example, C. J. Thompson compared the "socialized" and "academic" methods of teaching composition. While distinctions between the two methods extended beyond writing groups to include the context of writing, the nature of assignments, and focus of student attention, writing groups were an integral part of the socialized method. Thompson's empirical study revealed that students taught by the socialized method wrote with fewer mechanical errors and improved in writing skill faster than did students taught by the academic method.

Burges Johnson of Syracuse University conducted a related research project in the 1930s. Johnson compared the effects of the "experimental method" of teaching composition with one employing prose models to write about literature. The experimental method used writing groups almost exclusively. As Johnson describes it, the teacher joins students around a table in a circle so that each member faces the entire groups. "Students read their own writing aloud, listen to the criticism of fellow students, and a summing up by the instructor. Twenty-four students may be assembled in this way, with individual opportunity for each, provided the written assignments be brief. The reading of eight in a day would care for all in a week" (18). Johnson's study compared the effectiveness of these methods over a three-year period and found that students in the experimental classes consistently made the most improvement in writing. He explains: "The Experimental Method showed better results not only among the generality of its students but among the backward ones; better not only as to effective presentation of the writer's ideas, but also in the elimination of 'mechanical errors' of composition" (38).

Research carried out in recent years has yielded findings similar to those of Thompson and Johnson. Clifford found that students in writing groups made significantly greater gains on holistically scored writing samples than did their peers in traditional classes. Lagana's study demonstrated that writing groups enable students to improve critical thinking, organization, and appropriateness of writing, and Wayne found that mechanical aspects of writing improved when students worked in groups. Curiously, none of the recent research on writing groups acknowledges similar work done more than half a century ago.

Similarly, although hundreds of articles have been published about the pedagogy of writing groups since 1880, contemporary authors seem largely unaware of earlier work. In both 1919 and 1970 the word "experimental" appears in titles of articles about writing groups (Hedges; Putz). Both authors claim that writing groups increase motivation, foster critical thinking, enhance positive attitudes, and develop audience awareness, but Putz, like most contemporary writing group advocates, evinces no awareness of an earlier generation of writing groups. Writing in 1981, David James underlines the continuing obscurity of writing groups. He explains that he had for sixteen years written work read by teachers only and had continued the same practice in his own teaching until he learned about writing groups when he returned to graduate school. He notes that articles about peer critiques may appear in journals, but the topic remained unknown to him because "as acquainted as my English teachers may have been, they never let on, and I never learned how to write for anyone or anything but them and their artificial writing situations" (48). Echoes of this obscurity appear in surveys of high school students showing that a majority have never written for anyone but teachers (Applebee 88–89; Liftig 49). Writing groups may be a way of life for a certain percentage of teachers and students, but most have never experienced them.

Explanations for the relative obscurity of writing groups vary from the concrete to the theoretical. We can, for example, point to physical limitations, such as fixed desks, that until recently posed obstacles to introducing group work in schoolrooms. Alternatively, we can consider the common equation of writing groups with "progressive education." Most frequently associated with the name John Dewey, "progressive education" has been used to describe so many (and frequently conflicting) educational approaches that it carries multiple meanings; applying it to Dewey's complex theories is reductive. Dewey developed his theories at a time when a number of curricular movements emerged in this country, and while he drew from and contributed to several, his work cannot be contained by any of them. The subtlety and complexity of Dewey's theory of curriculum, enacted at the University of Chicago's Laboratory School during the early part of this century, extends far beyond terms such as "progressive education" or, worse, "learning by doing."

Likewise, "progressive education" adds little to our understanding of writing groups because its many definitions render it completely vague. Furthermore, "progressive education" is frequently used as a term of censure, and its very vagueness protects the traditionalist critic from interrogation, just as those who wish to undercut writing groups will, with a wave of the hand, dismiss them as "a phenomenon of the sixties," relying on the complexities of educational reform during that decade to block further discussion. To the extent, then, that writing groups are identified with progressive education they have been relegated to the sidelines because of the negative connotations attached to this term.

The more specific language of discrete philosophies offers another way to look at writing groups and at the same time explain their marginality. The movement of writing groups from student-sponsored organizations into the curricula of schools and colleges coincided with the emergence of several interest groups whose philosophies shaped curricula in this country. These interest groups include what Kliebard, in an effort to untangle some of the misapprehensions associated with progressive education, terms advocates of humanism, social meliorism, developmentalism, and social efficiency. Each contributed to writing groups, but their diversity, while enriching in many ways, blurred the intellectual focus of these groups.

Humanism, the most dominant of the four, was advocated by Harvard's President Charles Eliot, who served as chair of the National Education Association's Committee of Ten (a committee charged in 1892 with making curricular recommendations for high schools). He argued that all students, whether they were preparing for college or for "life," should take courses aimed at achieving humanist ideals of sensitivity to beauty, powers of reasoning, and high moral character. Although some of his followers were concerned by the ascendancy of the natural sciences and saw humanism as a way of preserving the cultural heritage implicit in literature, art, geography, mathematics, and history, Eliot himself was more concerned with enhancing critical reasoning skills. To this end, Eliot used his considerable influence to argue that education should foster systematic development of reasoning power. He wanted a student to be able to observe accurately, to classify and categorize, and to draw inferences, and thereby to be armed against "succumbing to the first plausible delusion or sophism he or she may encounter" (426).

Turn-of-the-century advocates such as Noyes and Tressler, who highlighted writing groups' capacity to foster critical thinking, manifested a humanist concern. In applauding students who become effective critics of their own and others' work, they aligned themselves with Eliot and other humanists who saw development of reasoning abilities at the heart of education. Descendants of this tradition participate in today's discussions of the relationship between core curricula and critical thinking. They frequently sit on committees of general education, and some of them advocate writing groups. Prominent among them is Kenneth Bruffee, who emphasizes writing groups' connection to intellectual growth. For Bruffee, writing groups involve "students in each other's intellectual, academic and social development" ("Brooklyn Plan" 447). Through carefully structured assignments and criteria for peer cricitism, students learn, claims Bruffee, to deal with ideas "not as artificial entities fully formed into an abstract and completed state . . . [but as] developing emanations of human beings' minds" ("Brooklyn Plan" 462). Bruffee's claims for the power of writing groups not only to improve writing but also to enhance students' mental capacities places him in the humanist tradition ("Collaborative Learning").

While humanists concentrate on improving individuals' minds, advocates of *social meliorism* seek to improve the world around them. Inspired by the work of botanist/geologist Lester Frank Ward, this tradition emerged to oppose the Social Darwinism popularized by Herbert Spencer's 1882 tour of the United States. While Social Darwinists argued that laws of natural selection applied to society, thereby justifying unequal distribution of wealth and power, the social meliorists took the position that because natural selection had produced intelligence, humans should use this intelligence to intervene and foster social progress. The force of these arguments derived from Ward's 1893 *Dynamic Sociology*, which argued for just distribution of education to achieve social progress, and from his *Psychic Factors of Civilization*, which claimed that nonpartisan governmental intervention on behalf of education would improve the human condition.

Those who noted writing groups' contributions to the development of all students, "not only among the generality of its students, but among the backward ones" (Johnson 38), followed the social meliorist line. Likewise, implicit in others' early-twentieth-century claims for writing groups' increasing cooperation and intelligent democracy is the social meliorist belief in fostering social progress for all (Aline Bright; Leonard "Two Types"). Ken Macrorie ties a contemporary form of social meliorism to writing groups as he argues that enfranchising students with the power of language will improve the world. His *Uptaught* opens with a description of students being arrested at a campus sit-in and indicts professors for making the university "sick unto death" by promulgating a "feel-nothing, say-nothing language" (18) called Engfish. Macrorie's alternative Third Way gives writing groups a central place. In *Writing to Be Read*, for example, he asserts that "a program for improving writing such as the one presented in this book will not succeed unless the beginning writer becomes experienced through engaging in critical sessions with his peers" (85). The terminology for writing groups varies across the three editions of this book, but "helping circles," as he eventually calls them, remain central to Macrorie's vision for schools. This vision emerges in full social meliorist form in the conclusion of *Uptaught*: "Out of the corner of my eye these days I sometimes see the glimmer of a world transformed by millions of persons who expect great things from each other" (187). Central to this transformation is the honest language that will, in Macrorie's view, emerge from writing groups. Although cloaked in 1960s terminology, Macrorie's equation of education with "a world transformed" shares much with Ward's insistence that schools could foster social progress.

While social meliorists of the 1890s drew upon the scientific views of Lester Frank Ward, *developmentalism* turned to the emerging field of psychology. It focused, in particular, on the work of G. Stanley Hall, author of *The Contents of Children's Minds on Entering School* (1893). Hall and others active in the child-study movement observed and recorded children's behavior to provide a more scientific description of human development. They argued that education should be shaped to conform to this development, but they stopped short of insisting on standardization because they believed in acknowledging individual differences. Although it took several forms, the "laboratory method" described by early advocates of writing groups reflected developmentalist assumptions because it individualized education and allowed for a wider range of development than did more traditional classes.

In the intervening years cognitive psychologists have built upon investigations initiated by nineteenth-century developmentalists. Notable among them is Jean Piaget, whose study of intellectual growth in children yielded descriptions of "concrete operations" and "formal operations," terms now familiar to nearly all educators. In his *Teaching the Universe of Discourse*, James Moffett proposes a "pedagogical theory of discourse" based on the stages of intellectual development described by Piaget. Moffett accepts Piaget's view that decreased egocentrism accompanies intellectual growth, and he describes a progression of discourse to fit this growth. Echoes of nineteenth-century developmentalism sound in Moffett's claim that: "A child is not an empty vessel when he enters school" (24) and that "the most sensible strategy for determining a proper learning order in English . . . is to look for the main lines of child development and to assimilate to them, when fitting, the various formulations that scholars make about language and literature" (14).

Writing groups dominate Moffett's developmental scheme because they provide what he calls "feedback," a response analogous to that which helps children learn to talk. He explains: "Learning to use language, then, requires the particular feedback of human response, because it is to other people that we direct speech. The fact that one writes by oneself does not at all diminish the need for response, since one writes for others" (191). In Moffett's terms, the responses of writing groups foster intellectual development because they help students learn to move beyond egocentrism to take the perspectives of others, or as he puts it, to move "from the center of the self outward" (59).

The fourth legacy of the late nineteenth century, the social efficiency tradition, attempted to adapt scientific systems of management to education. Lacking the intellectual basis of humanism, social meliorism, and developmentalism, this tradition drew on methods successful in business. Typical of these, the Taylor method, credited to an engineer named Frederick Taylor, measured business success in profits. Franklin Bobbitt, an instructor in educational administration, claimed that efficiency principles of clarifying goals and eliminating waste could be applied to education as easily as to business. He asserted that the tasks of management, direction, and supervision remained constant across fields and that educational success could be measured in terms of skilled and productive graduates.

A major figure in importing social efficiency into education was Joseph Mayer Rice, a pediatrician who left his practice to survey what actually occurred in schools. The book containing his reports attacked school administrators, school boards, and the general public for giving too little attention to their schools, and it censured teachers for incompetence. Rice's first book, *The Public School System of the United States* (1893), generated great controversy among educators, but Rice persisted in his surveys to determine why students at one school achieved more than those at another. These surveys resulted in his *Scientific Management in Education*, in which Rice argued that teachers should adopt a "scientific system of pedagogical management" (xiv) that would measure results in terms of fixed standards.

Rice's educational plan specified that students should develop basic skills. He and his followers took exception to the view that basic skills were merely tools of knowledge, arguing instead that "the citizen who is not properly grounded in the three R's labors at a disadvantage in the struggle for existence" (24). Skill was important to theorists of social efficiency, and skill in writing figured prominently in their hierarchy of value. Concern with efficiency appears with some frequency in early discussions of writing groups, particularly efficiency in making students more skillful writers. Buck and Woodbridge, for example, opened their 1899 text with the claim that "the English teacher, more perhaps than any other, is conscious of aiming, not to give his students information, but to make them acquire capacity, capacity in this case, for expressing their thoughts to others" (iii) and went on to advocate writing groups because they provide student writers a 'real' audience.

In contemporary terms, social efficiency manifests itself in pressures toward defining behavioral objectives, returning to "the basics," and eliminating waste in education. Writing group enthusiasts who belong or respond to the social efficiency tradition marshall terms such as *basics*, (Liftig), *grammar* (Kuykendall) and *skills* to describe peer critiques. The term *skills* appears frequently in the first edition of Donald Murray's *A Writer Teaches Writing*, and although Murray cannot be described as an advocate of social efficiency, his background in journalism probably contributes to the suggestion of social efficiency in his work. The preface to Murray's first edition promises to show "how the skills of the publishing writer can be learned by the student. The ability to write is not a gift, it is a skill" (xi). In the first chapter Murray identifies seven skills necessary to writing and offers this rationale: "We teach the student to write because he has to be a writer, revealing his knowledge to his teachers before he is allowed to graduate. Once the student becomes a working member of our complex society he will probably write reports, letters, proposals, memoranda, in order to work with people beyond his office and his community" (1). Joseph Mayer Rice would surely agree.

Murray claims that students can learn skills of writing if teachers create a proper instructional climate, and writing groups contribute to this climate. Like writing group supporters of fifty years ago, Murray describes the writing class as a "laboratory," one where "small groups of students can work editing each other's papers" (110). In such an environment, according to Murray, students can discover and practice the "writer's basic skills" (1).

These four currents—humanism, social meliorism, developmentalism, and social efficiency—each contributed to the development of writing groups, and they continue to shape thinking about these groups today. Beneath these currents, closer to the ecosphere of the English classroom, flowed smaller rivulets that likewise influenced writing groups. One of these was the work and influence of Fred Newton Scott (the earlier mentioned member of the "Big Four"), professor of rhetoric at the University of Michigan from 1889 to 1927. At a time when thinking about English composition was dominated by the Harvard Reports of 1892, 1895, and 1897, and their concern with correctness, Scott took the position that the "almost universal practice of teaching composition by pointing out to the writer the errors in his themes" ("English Composition" 463) wasted time and should be replaced by an attempt to unite the symbolic system of writing with students' inherent "ideas of sociability" (471).

Because of his background in classical rhetoric, Scott sought to establish a fuller conception of rhetoric, one extending to issues of audience and purpose. This fuller conception should, he argued, shape both the teaching and evaluation of writing. As Albert Kitzhaber has noted, Scott was the only original thinker among the prominent rhetoricians of his time (Adams Sherman Hill, John Genung, and Barrett Wendell being the others), but, despite Scott's efforts, "the narrower philosophy of the Harvard group won out, with the result that rhetorical instruction in America until well into the 1930s became, for all practical purposes, little more than instruction in grammar and the mechanics of writing, motivated almost solely by the ideal of superficial correctness" (120).

Narrow conceptions of writing dominated, but Scott's influence persisted through his texts and through the students he trained. Scott's social view of writing, in particular, lent support to writing groups. Scott and his co-author Joseph Denney wrote texts for composition classes at all grade levels, and these books gave prominence to the social dimension of writing. In *Elementary English*, for example, Scott and Denney urge instructors to make pupils aware of "the 'other man' for whom they are writing" (iii), and suggestions throughout the text reinforce this statement.

Scott's students echoed and enlarged upon his concern with the social aspect of writing, and they recommended writing groups as one way to enhance it. Gertrude Buck, a student of Scott's who taught at Vassar, opened her *Course in Expository Writing* (co-authored with Elisabeth Woodbridge) by acknowledging the problem of students who are expected to write without an audience: "He [the student] feels 'silly'. . . . or at least uncomfortable. But give him somebody to talk to, a real audience, and a subject that his audience is interested in, and his whole attitude will change" (iv). This admonition reflects Scott's concern that writing be conceived of in social terms. Writing groups, according to the authors, provide one way to give students a real audience: "When the students have written on one of the subjects, let each read a fellow student's paper and try to give back to him in other language exactly the impression it conveys. On this basis—that of its effect on its audience—the writer may then rework his description" (48).

A 1917 textbook, *English Composition as a Social Problem* by Sterling Leonard, another of Scott's students, emphasizes concern with social considerations in writing. Leonard describes three processes ("processes" is his word) for elementary school composition students. The first prepares students for writing, and the third deals with organization. The second, "following the child's presentation of an oral or written theme[,] is criticism by all the class of each one's work to show its values and to suggest how it could be better done" (44). Leonard advocates, thereby, a writing group wherein students attempt "specific evaluation" (47). He acknowledges that students may experience initial difficulty making effective evaluations but explains that the main purpose of this method is to help students "develop principles of criticism" (50). As indicated in the Bibliography, both Buck and Leonard published articles about writing groups in addition to recommending them in textbooks.

Although he was not a University of Michigan student, George Carpenter, professor of composition and rhetoric at Columbia, also came under Scott's influence. In his *Elements of Rhetoric and Composition* Carpenter acknowledges both his personal debt and that of composition studies generally to Scott. True to his mentor, Carpenter recommends writing groups, exhorting members to "criticize the composition of one of your classmates, pointing out the places where, if at all, his work is lacking in coherence, and showing how the fault could be remedied" (208). He continues: "Criticize the plan of a composition by one of your classmates, pointing out every point where it is unnecessarily vague" (228). In statements such as these Carpenter reflects Scott's concern with emphasizing the social dimension in writing.

Reformers of the Fred Newton Scott school experienced their greatest successes in elementary schools rather than in high schools or colleges. Texts such as Buck's and Woodbridge's and Leonard's were written for and used by elementary school classes. There were, to be sure, some advocates of writing groups in high school and college classes, but the majority were teachers of young children.

The receptivity of elementary schools to curricular reform has been well documented. In his investigation of teaching practices in the 1920s and 1930s, Larry Cuban found that the highest percentage of innovation (defined by Cuban as student-centered practices) occurred in primary grades (200). Innovations appeared much less frequently in intermediate grades and were often completely absent in high schools. Although Cuban's investigation does not focus on them exclusively, the innovations he describes include writing groups. William Woods, in tracing the history of nineteenth-century composition teaching, identifies elementary schools as centers of the most active reform. He explains that, unlike high schools, elementary schools were not charged with disciplining students' minds, nor did they have to prepare students for standardized college entrance requirements. Rather, they were to prepare minds for future learning. Elementary schools therefore emphasized the practice and activity of learning rather than the specific content central to higher grades. In addition, elementary schools, to a greater degree than high schools or colleges, were influenced by reformist ideas emanating from social and economic expansions of the mid-nineteenth century and by continental theorists such as Johann Pestalozzi.

Accordingly, elementary schools provided a hospitable environment for the growth of student-centered practices such as writing groups. The "informal" classes Donald Graves identifies in his 1975 report on elementary school composition instruction testify to the longevity of this reform tradition. Characterizing "informal" classes as those permitting students greater freedom to function without teacher direction and to determine their own learning activities, Graves, a contemporary advocate of writing groups for elementary school children, distinguishes them from "formal" or traditional teacher-directed classes (239). Now, as during the nineteenth century, many elementary school classrooms provide students opportunities to read and respond to one another's writing.

Scott and his followers were eclipsed by those who equated writing with correct forms, but this sturdy band helped writing groups endure. The small but steady list of publications recorded in the Bibliography for the years between 1900 and the late 1960s demonstrates their success. No doubt a number of these authors employed writing groups because of Scott's direct or indirect influence. Scott and those persuaded by his arguments contributed to writing groups, as did the larger movements of humanism, social meliorism, developmentalism, and social efficiency. The diversity of these movements and individual contributions nourished writing groups but, ironically, also prevented writing groups from developing a base solid enough to support them in the educational mainstream.

Writing groups persisted without flourishing for the first five decades of this century. They remained relatively marginal until a series of events pressured their diverse institutional and intellectual sources into a new configuration. The 1966 Dartmouth Conference constituted one of these events. This gathering of British and American educators initiated dialogue between adherents to two different views of English instruction. After World War II and especially during the post-Sputnik era, English teaching in the United States had been reformed by the academic model of Yale's "tripod" of language, literature, and composition. Between 1958 and 1966 curricular reform in English emphasized content dictated by this tripod. At the 1966 Dartmouth Conference, American educators active in this emerging academic reform movement confronted British instructors for whom student response was more important than close reading of literature, tentativeness more valued than precise formulation in language, and process more significant than product in writing. While Americans had been engaged in academic reform, British educators had been moving in a different direction. Influenced by the work of Jean Piaget, Lev Vygotsky, and George Kelly, English studies in Britain had developed a model grounded in students' personal and linguistic development.

American response to the British model was positive and swift. In the years immediately after 1966, English studies in this country abandoned much of its tripod-based academic reform in favor of a curriculum emulating that of the British. Not surprisingly, writing groups flourished in the changed educational climate. In 1968 alone, three books advocating writing groups—Ken Macrorie's *Writing to Be Read*, James Moffett's *Teaching the Universe of Discourse*, and Donald Murray's *A Writer Teaches Writing*—were published. Each of these books addressed a different audience. Macrorie wrote for instructors of college composition classes, Moffett for elementary school children, and Murray for high school teachers. Thus, although none of these books became a best-seller, together they reached a wide population. As the earlier discussion of educational theories demonstrated, Macrorie, Moffett, and Murray each had a slightly different perspective on writing groups. Ken Macrorie urged honesty in writing and described "helping circles" as a place where writers could learn to hear their own language better. Donald Murray's concern with the skills of writing led him to see the classroom as a laboratory where students could work together to emulate the practices and successes of professional writers. James Moffett's interest in cognitive development led him to emphasize students' need to envision audiences for their writing, a need met by teachers who "break the class into groups . . . to exchange papers . . . write comments on them, and discuss them" (197).

As the earlier discussion of 1890s curricular reforms reveals, the Macrorie-social meliorism, Moffett-developmentalism, and Murray-social efficiency similarities show that the various movements that shaped writing groups were not new in 1968. The Dartmouth Conference and its aftermath did not cause writing groups to emerge; it merely realigned subterranean forces to bring them closer to the surface. The intellectual climate of 1968 was more hospitable to writing groups than that of previous decades because, as will be discussed in chapters 3 and 4, views of the nature of knowledge had begun to shift.

The Bibliography shows that three times more articles on writing groups were published in the 1970s than in either of the two preceding decades. Some of this increase can be attributed to the appearance of new journals and the growing strength of *College Composition and Communication*, a journal inaugurated in 1950, but even allowing for increases in the number and strength of journals, the fact remains that writing groups have attracted considerably more attention in the past two decades than during any earlier period. Books followed the same pattern, with successive editions (of Macrorie and, in the 1980s, Murray) and additional titles, notably Peter Elbow's *Writing without Teachers* (1973), joining the publication bulge.

The establishment of the National Writing Project (NWP) also contributed to writing groups' new prominence. Originated in 1974 as the Bay Area Writing Project, an inservice training program for composition instructors, the NWP emerged as a confederacy of more than 100 sites scattered across the country by 1984. Membership in the confederacy required, among other things, that teachers-in-training write and participate in writing groups. James Gray, director and founder of the Project, imported this requirement from his own teaching, and alumni of the NWP likewise have brought writing groups to their own classes (Gere and Abbott; Mason; Peckham; Sears). Exact figures remain elusive, but in 1984 the NWP trained more than 70,000 teachers in a single year ("Evaluation Portfolio" 4). Each of these teachers participated in a writing group, and a substantial number later introduced writing groups in their own classes. If we assume that the NWP trained approximately 350,000 teachers over a five-year period and that at least 30 percent of them subsequently began using writing groups in their own classes, then the number of students participating in writing groups as a direct result of the NWP approaches three million. These figures are impressive and may call statements about the relative marginality of writing groups into question until we note that the United States has approximately 2.2 million teachers of grades one through twelve, where the NWP has concentrated its efforts (although the NWP does work with college instructors, that population remains extremely small), which means that the 300,000 figure represents less than 15 percent of this country's teachers.

More subtle and less quantifiable but equally influential are the recent critiques of writing groups. These examinations vary in tone. Some, such as Higley's parody of a desultory session of distractable and unmotivated students and Cantwell's flippant advice that writing groups harbor potential chaos and should not be used in the spring, merely wink at substantive issues. Others, however, elicit serious thought. Thomas Newkirk, for example, asks profound questions about the interpretive communities engendered by writing groups and how they shape both students' and teachers' understanding of evaluation; Harvey Kail raises questions about the compatibility of circular and recursive writing-group work with more traditional linear models of education; and Carol Berkenkotter provokes readers to rethink how writing groups can impinge upon the writer's authority over a text.

Challenging as these questions are, their ultimate significance lies not in the responses they generate but in their very existence. This shifting away from the unanimous chorus of affirmation—from enthusiastic instructors, sympathetic theorists, studies illustrating their benefits—signals a new maturity. When a practice merits thoughtful critique as well as generalized enthusiasm, it has come of age. The conglomerate of literary societies and classroom adaptations has wound its way through intellectual traditions both within and beyond English studies, culminating in writing groups that preserve old traditions and incorporate new adaptations as they become increasingly visible in the educational skyline.

2

Writing Groups outside Academic Institutions

SEVENTEENTH- AND EIGHTEENTH-CENTURY COLLEGE STUDENTS drew on faculty and institutional support as they organized and participated in literary societies. Resources of time, space, and intellect were readily available as students gathered to acquire "something of intellectual culture." Many persons outside academic institutions shared their interest in enhancing intellect but had to rely on themselves to create opportunities for fostering it. They contributed to this country's long tradition of self-help by creating groups outside academia. The mutual improvement societies formed by these self-reliant men and women differed as did the histories of males and females during the first two centuries after Europeans arrived on the North American continent. Despite their differences, men's and women's mutual improvement societies shared many common features, chief among them one also prominent in college literary societies—a considerable interest in writing.

Like college literary societies, mutual improvement groups extend back to colonial times. Benjamin Franklin, who had only two years of formal education, was among the first to initiate such a group. When he was still in his teens, Franklin and his friends Charles Osborne, Joseph Watson, and James Ralph met frequently to share ideas and occasionally to "produce a piece of our own composing, in order to improve it by our mutual observations, criticisms, and corrections" (Goodman 78). This relatively informal group was later replaced by Franklin's Junto, a club "established for mutual improvement" in 1728 (Goodman 315). Members of the

Junto met on Friday evenings to discuss their reading, experiences, and current events. Among the requirements was that each member should "once in three months produce and read an essay of his own writing on any subject he pleased" (Goodman 98). Improving writing through sharing it with peers thus took a prominent place in the earliest mutual improvement efforts.

Franklin's Junto presaged a long line of self-improvement groups. Two qualities described by social historians as distinctly American underlay these groups: an egalitarian view of knowledge and an impulse toward joining with others to initiate change. As Daniel Boorstin has explained, a "new concept of knowledge" (150) developed in America. Unlike societies of western Europe where the "explaining" classes controlled knowledge, "American life quickly proved uncongenial to any special class of 'knowers.' Men here were more interested in the elaboration of experience than in the elaboration of 'truth'" (Boorstin 150). Unlike their European counterparts who were "denied freedom of discovery," who "depended on the monumental accomplishments of the few," and who could "show good sense only by acting according to ways approved by their 'betters,'" the new culture of the United States, "diffused, elusive, process-oriented—depended more on the novel" (Boorstin 150). In summary, "Out of all the limitations and opportunities of colonial American grew an American ideal, which sprang from the conviction that knowledge, like the New World itself, was still only half-discovered" (Boorstin 188). Because Americans saw knowledge as the property of all rather than a select few, they did not hesitate to seek it on their own without benefit of formalized institutions. Accordingly, instead of lamenting the inaccessibility of higher education, many Americans undertook to educate themselves.

Impulses toward cooperation accompanied this egalitarian view of knowledge. Early Americans had an unusually strong tendency to gather together on issues of mutual concern. Henry Steele Commager describes the early-nineteenth-century citizen this way: "For all his individualism, the American was much given to cooperative undertakings and to joining. Nowhere else except in Britain did men associate so readily for common purposes; nowhere else were private associations so numerous or so efficacious. . . . As the American had created his church and his state, he took for granted his capacity to create all lesser institutions and associations" (22). Mutual improvement societies modeled after Franklin's Junto numbered among the "lesser associations" frequently created. From colonial times forward groups of people gathered in cities and in small towns to educate themselves. Self-education groups frequently employed lectures and debates, but writing also played an important role. Groups of young men, like Franklin and his friends, gathered into "young men's associations" to inform one another about various topics. In Kennebunk, Maine, for example, a group of young men formed a club in 1829, and five of them agreed to deliver lectures. The first was on self-education, three were on science, and the fifth was on the early history of the town (Bode 58). In New Haven, Connecticut, a group of workingmen formed a group called the Apprentices' Literary Association in 1826. Members offered one another instruction in arithmetic, geometry, geography, grammar, and bookkeeping (Bode 58). Writing figured in these young men's associations as it had in earlier self-improvement groups. When members prepared lectures, they frequently wrote the substance of their talk, and the discussion/critique following lectures provided authors a discussion of the form and substance of their writing much as Franklin's Junto did.

The growth of these self-improvement groups indicates something of their value. In 1833, Boston alone claimed at least eleven young men's associations with more than 1500 members. These groups, like young men's associations elsewhere in the country, took as their purpose "elevating the minds and purifying the hearts of mankind, and thus laying the broad foundation of national prosperity" (Amasa Walker 123). Their goal of improving the common mind built on the egalitarian principle "that it is far better to have the many well informed than the few learned" (Amasa Walker 124). For the Boston groups, which met one evening a month, writing constituted the major activity. Individuals or groups wrote reports on local issues such as gambling, intemperance, theaters, and slavery. These reports were read at meetings, and subsequent discussions of them frequently led to resolutions by the association. As the topics suggest, moral development joined intellectual growth on the list of association goals, and the one criterion of membership was "a good character" (Amasa Walker 126).

Writing and the other intellectual activities of these associations enabled young men to assume positions of leadership in their communities. A speaker of the time noted: "Moral and political power are no longer concentrated in the ranks of the grey-haired and care-wrinkled. They have settled towards the base of society, and are now wielded more fully perhaps by the class whose ages extend from twenty years to six and thirty, than by any other" (Amasa Walker 122). This democratizing extended to class as well as age because young men's associations enabled those from "less fashionable" backgrounds to improve their status.

The largest and most successful mutual improvement groups evolved from the Lyceum movement. Modeled after the British Mechanics' Institution, the first Lyceum started in 1826, under the direction of Josiah Holbrook. This society for mutual education had two objectives: (1) to "procure for youths an economical and practical education, and to diffuse rational and useful information through the community generally"; and (2) "to apply the sciences and various branches of education to the domestic and useful arts, and to all the common purposes of life" (Bode 12). Writing figured in Lyceum work because the small groups organized for learning provided a forum, much as the young men's associations before them had, wherein members had opportunities to read their own writing and listen to that of others.

Frequently, as happened with the New Haven Apprentices Literary Association, existing mutual improvement societies were incorporated into the Lyceum system. Numbers indicate the effect of the Lyceum system, an organization that Holbrook organized to have local, county, state, and national boards. In 1829, two years after the first Lyceum was organized in Millbury, Massachusetts, there were one hundred Lyceums. By 1834 there were 3000 in fifteen states, and in the 1840s "every state had Lyceums which not only sponsored lectures but maintained libraries and museums, organized classes and published teaching materials" (Nye 360). Farther west, in Ohio, for example, the Lyceum movement flourished in the 1850s, and here, as elsewhere, prosperous groups hired prominent lecturers while the less affluent majority relied upon the eloquence of its own membership (Mead 179). Even when lecturers were hired, their charge was not so much to impart information as to "stimulate men to individual effort, to induce thought and discussion" (Mead 19). Self-improvement, in the Lyceum view, required individual effort, and a considerable amount of this effort involved writing.

Membership in a college literary society did not preclude participation in self-sponsored groups, and it may have encouraged it. Young men who knew the benefits of giving and receiving critiques on writing frequently sought other opportunities for the same. William Hammond, whose diary records his undergraduate experience at Amherst from 1846 to 1848, belonged to Academia, a literary society where reading and responding to members' writing constituted a major part of the literary exercises. In addition to descriptions of writing read in Academia, Hammond's diary includes frequent mention of extra-Academia meetings, in dormitories or rooming houses, where a few young men met and "read our compositions and criticized each other[']s" (64).

The Civil War disrupted the Lyceum system, and although some groups survived into the latter part of the nineteenth century, the institution had, as Bode notes, "ended with the Civil War" (252). The Lyceum system disappeared, but its progeny took at least two forms: one, the continuation of mutual improvement societies; and the other, the development of the public lecture series. The most widespread and all-encompassing of the progeny was the Chautauqua movement. Chautauqua's founders concerned themselves with religious education, but they took a broad view of the similarities between secular and religious learning (Vincent 12–13). Like the Lyceum system, the Chautauqua movement educated its followers through lectures, but it departed from the Lyceum by holding large summer assemblies in addition to sponsoring small study groups.

New York State inaugurated a summer assembly in 1874, but replicas soon appeared in other parts of the country, creating a Chautauqua circuit. The Chautauqua Literary and Science Circle fostered writing groups by providing a course of study to be followed by small groups meeting independently throughout the year, and these groups frequently wrote and read papers as part of their year's work. A number of the women's groups I will discuss later evolved from Chautauqua circles (Croly 363, 383, 472). Americans welcomed the Chautauqua model of self-education by expanding its circuit to 562 municipalities in 1921, and the Chautauqua Literary and Science Circle, which was formed in 1878, claimed more than 100,000 members by 1891 (Orchard 189).

Chautauqua exerted qualitative as well as quantitative influence. As one commentator wrote, it prevented "education from becoming an aristocracy among a favored few" (Orchard 52). Those who benefitted from formal education at both high school and college levels indeed constituted a "favored few" during this period and well into the middle of the next century. In 1870, for example, 2% of all seventeen-year-olds in the United States graduated from high school, and approximately 50% of this group (or 1% of the seventeen-year-olds) went on to attain a college degree. In 1900 6.3% of seventeen-year-olds graduated from high school and 36% of this group received a college degree four years later. It was not until 1948 that a majority (52.3%) of seventeen-year-olds in this country graduated from high school, and approximately 27% of them subsequently graduated from college (United States, 386). At a time when few received extensive formal education, Chautauqua provided an alternative. It helped preserve, in other words, colonial America's egalitarian view of knowledge and its impulse to join in cooperative ventures. Institutionalized forms of self-education such as the Lyceum and Chautauqua lent other self-sponsored groups the confidence to initiate or continue their own efforts at mutual improvement. Extra-academic writing groups initiated as part of institutionalized self-education programs survived the demise of these programs because the spirit of self-education outlived the institution that nurtured it.

As the foregoing discussion indicates, self-improvement societies remained, until the middle of the nineteenth century, largely male provinces. True, women could attend some Lyceum groups, but only if accompanied by their male relatives, and Josiah Holbrook's original design for the Lyceum put young male apprentices and clerks at the center (Bode 12). Women had no legitimate place in these societies any more than they had a place in higher education. Reasons for excluding women from mutual improvement societies and from higher education varied across time, but the fact of exclusion remained constant until the middle of the nineteenth century. Accordingly, women's self-improvement groups have their own history.

During colonial times, the small corps of available women received considerable social pressure to marry and produce children, and women contributed directly to family and national economies by producing food, cloth, and clothing in their homes. These domestic duties occupied women so fully that they had little time for self-improvement of any sort. The limited opportunities for women's self-sponsored education prior to the mid nineteenth century centered on the church, where women gathered in small groups for Bible study. Because these gatherings were so informal, recordings of their proceedings were ephemeral, and we have no way of knowing what occurred. It seems safe to assume however, that little writing was done in these groups. As factories took over spinning and weaving in the 1840s, society developed a new rationale for isolating white middle-class women in their homes: they were defined as spiritual and moral ladies responsible for protecting domestic purity, a purity threatened by contact with the world. Minority and poor women might work as servants or toil in factories, but the emerging code of "ladydom" (Welter) required middle-class women to remain in their homes.

Rationales for restricting middle-class women to the domestic sphere came from both medicine and theology. To be "delicate" or "sickly" was often a term of praise for women, and as late as 1858 the popular press asserted that "the fact is certain the American girl is a very delicate plant . . . not generally strong in nerve and muscle, and too ready to fade before her true mid-summer has come" (Woody 105). Physicians supported this view by claiming biological deficiencies for women, deficiencies that made extradomestic activities dangerous for them. Too much mental exertion, like too much physical strain, would push them beyond their endurance. Members of the clergy emphasized women's moral purity and urged them to avoid defiling it with worldly things. The "Pastoral Letter" issued by the General Association of Massachusetts preachers in 1837 stated that the proper "duties and influence of women are clearly stated in the New Testament [and are] unobtrusive and private. . . . The power of woman is her dependence, flowing from the consciousness of that weakness which God has given for her protection, and which keeps her in those departments of life that form the character of individuals, and of the nation" (Woody 423).

These arguments kept white middle-class women at home through much of the nineteenth century. They might attend a Lyceum or, later, a Chautuaqua with fathers, husbands, or brothers, but they were actively discouraged from forming self-improvement groups of their own. Likewise, women were barred from higher education through much of the nineteenth century. Opponents argued that education was wasted on women because their roles did not require it. In 1836, for example, a fund raiser for a women's college was re-buffed by this response: "No, I will not give you a dollar; all that a woman needs to know is how to read the New Testament, and to spin and weave clothing for her family. . . . I would not have one of your graduates for a wife, and I will not give you a cent for any such ob-ject" (Woody 152). A variation on this position argued that women wasted their educations by marrying. "After your college girl has graduated, she may, possibly, spend three years in teaching. By that time she is tolerably certain to marry. And then what becomes of her higher education?" (Woody 152). As late as 1894, popular journals argued that college education "may have excellencies for men. . . . for women it can only be hardening and deforming" (Woody 152). Even educators who supported higher education for women took the position that this education should take a distinctly different form. Samuel Thurber, for example, wrote: "For the women to copy men's examinations and competitions, especially such competitive schemes as have developed themselves in the upper education of England, is, it seems to me, to go altogether and disastrously wrong" ("English Literature" 335).

Population shifts called into question the popular mythology about women's domestic destiny. By the middle of the nineteenth century, men were in the minority in several eastern states, and "What shall we do with the superfluous women?" became the ques-tion (Woody 1). One response was to establish separate and unequal higher education in the form of academies and seminaries for women. The Troy Female Academy opened in 1821, the Hartford Female Academy in 1823, and Mount Holyoke Seminary in 1837. These in-stitutions eschewed the traditional classical curriculum offered by men's colleges of the time, providing, instead, preparation in domes-tic arts and socially valued "accomplishments" in art and music. Some of the women trained in academies and seminaries did teach— teaching was the only career open to women until 1850—but aca-demies and seminaries did not provide the professional training for medicine, law, and ministry available in men's colleges of the same period.

Despite their limited educational value, women's academies and seminaries did open the way for more education, both institutionalized and self-sponsored, for women. As the general population became more receptive to the idea of educated women, it likewise became more tolerant of self-improvement groups for women. By 1855, much of society had accepted the idea of college education for young women, in institutions like those established for men, and efforts had been made to establish such institutions in all regions of the United States. Coeducation likewise became more widely accepted. Oberlin College opened as the first coeducational institution in 1833, but kept the female department separate for a number of years and did not actually award degrees to women until the 1840s. A decade later, however, many colleges and universities educated women and men together. Coeducation was particularly strong in midwestern and western state universities. Among the state universities enrolling women from their founding were Utah (1850), Iowa (1856), Kansas (1860), and Nebraska (1871); Wisconsin, Indiana, Missouri, Michigan, Ohio State, Illinois, and California all admitted women in the 1860s.

The expansion of institutionalized higher education for women opened the way for more powerful and widespread self-improvement groups. The same social forces that had resisted higher education for women also created obstacles to women's self-improvement groups. Prior to 1855 most middle-class women's social acceptability depended upon their remaining isolated at home, upholding the code of "ladydom." There were, of course, a few exceptions. Church-sponsored Bible study groups freed women for mutual improvement while keeping them within the socially approved role of fostering morality.

A few secular groups also formed during the early nineteenth century. Women in Chelsea, Connecticut, founded a literary society in 1800 to "enlighten the understanding and expand the ideas of its members and to promote useful knowledge" (Blair 12), and Elizabeth Buffum Chase belonged to a Female Mutual Improvement Society in New England prior to the Civil War, a group in which members met weekly to read books and "exchange original compositions" (Chase 31). Chase explained her need for this group: "I knew every rule in the [Murray] grammar, but I did not know how to apply one of them to the first word" (23–24). Such groups did not attract a significant number of women, however, until educated females were more widely accepted than they had been during the early nineteenth century. Accordingly, the major growth of women's clubs occurred after 1865.

During the late nineteenth century, after educated women were tolerated but before they had been enfranchised as voting citizens or as legitimate professionals, clubs enabled women to develop intellectually. As Karen Blair has demonstrated, the domestic feminism of literary clubs offered women of the nineteenth century a way to "leave the confines of the home without abandoning domestic values" (4). While men might occasionally rail that clubs led to a decreased output of homemade pies (Blair 70), women could participate in clubs without risking social disapproval. In fact, women could explain mental improvement engendered by literary clubs as consonant with rather than in opposition to their domestic roles. That is, women who discussed and wrote about religion or (even) literature and art in clubs would be more effective moral guardians of their homes.

The express purposes (and many of the activities) of women's clubs resembled those of young men's college-sponsored literary societies and mutual improvement societies. Names such as "The Monday Afternoon Club" or "The Fortnightly" or "Progressive Culture Club" or "The Century Club" designated groups of women who banded together to make themselves "acquainted with the best in literature and art, the best of the past, the best in the present" (Croly 220), "to promote the highest intellectual development of its members" (Croly 364), and "to consider questions relating to the moral, intellectual, and social improvement of women" (Croly 547). Women's clubs frequently carried out literary exercises similar to those of college literary clubs, but the political motivations behind women's groups differed. For nineteenth-century women, literary clubs provided one of the few socially acceptable alternatives to domestic isolation, while for young male students it constituted one of several forms of self-enrichment.

Writing played an important role in women's clubs for intellectual, economic, and political reasons. Two of the earliest women's clubs illustrate this role. Journalist Jane Cunningham Croly founded

Sorosis in New York City in 1868 after having been denied admission to a Charles Dickens reading held at the Press Club. Feeling that women needed an organization of their own if they were to be excluded by men, Croly convened a group interested in improving women's status. Like Croly, many of the members had careers in writing, but the club was not composed of writers exclusively. By avoiding specific reform movements and concentrating on the general issue of self-help and personal growth, Sorosis avoided most of the social stigma attached to more radical women's suffrage groups.

The political impetus for founding Sorosis centered on writing. Professional women writers who were denied admission to meetings of their male peers needed an organization of their own. But intellectual motivations were also important, and they too focused on writing. Sorosis sought members "hungry for the society of women, that is, for the society of those whose deeper natures had been roused to activity, who had been seized by the divine spirit of inquiry and aspiration, who were interested in the thought and progress of the age, and in what other women were thinking and doing" (Croly 7). Writing and presenting papers to the club addressed the intellectual hunger of its members.

The New England Women's Club, also founded in 1868, harbored somewhat less political motivation because it numbered fewer career women among its membership; but it shared Sorosis's intellectual impetus. Its stated purpose included this declaration: "Its plan involves no special pledge to any one form of activity, but implies only a womanly interest in all true thought and effort on behalf of women, and of society in general, for which women are so largely responsible" (Blair 32). Like Sorosis, the New England Women's Club answered concerns for cultural advancement with a regular schedule of papers presented by members or by invited guests. And like all women's clubs, the New England Women's Club served political ends as it accomplished its intellectual goals. The process of writing and presenting papers gave women experience and confidence, thereby preparing them for other forms of public life.

Writing a paper and reading it at a club meeting terrified most women, but this experience carried economic advantages as well as political and intellectual ones. Despite the stereotypical view of women as helpless and indulged domestic creatures, many middle class women turned to writing in economic distress. As Ann Wood notes, many women writers of the nineteenth century "were widows, suddenly forced to support themselves and their children, or women otherwise unexpectedly robbed of male support" (9). Few careers were open to women, and those that were—such as teaching—paid women less than the paltry sum received by their male counterparts. Whether as a sole source of support or as a supplement to a meager income, writing offered nineteenth-century women a measure of economic security, and clubs provided a training ground and/or support group for many women writers.

Like Sorosis and the New England Women's Club, the women's clubs that sprang up across the country followed the model of requiring members to present papers. As Karen Blair explains, "There are no reliable figures on the total number of women who joined literary clubs during the second half of the nineteenth century, but many thousands of women found refuge in the dozens of clubs that formed in almost every city, town and village in the country" (61–62). The General Federation of Women's Clubs initiated in 1890 united many of these clubs under a single national organization, but the shape of club activities had already been established. Like the Chicago Women's Club, founded in 1876, clubs held "exercises consisting of a paper and discussion, the different departments [departments such as reform, home, education, philanthropy, art and literature, philosophy, and science] taking turns in supplying the topic and essayist of the day" (Croly 62). Club members valued these papers, and many, like the Seattle Women's Century Club, which claimed that "one original paper a year was extracted from each member," preserved them: "Papers read before the club will become the property of the club, and a fair copy on sermon paper must be filed with the Corresponding Secretary."

Frequently club members would decide on a course of study and assign papers a year in advance. Women were then responsible for writing essays on topics such as "History of the Jesuits," "Commercial Influence of the Netherlands," "French Revolution of 1789" (Croly 56), "Physical Education of Women," "The Geography of Russia," "Frontier Experiences," and "Medieval Sculpture" (Wednesday P.M. Club of Seattle). Regardless of whether they had attended a college or an academy or no institution of higher education, women found these papers a major undertaking and did extensive research to prepare them. As had been true for men in college literary societies, club women frequently had little or no access to books, so they created their own libraries. In 1933 the American Library Association credited women's clubs with initiating 75 percent of the public libraries in the United States (Blair 100–101). Women's clubs also reached into their communities through schools, and their work in writing and literature made members especially interested in the English curriculum. Not uncommonly, therefore, members of women's clubs made recommendations about writing in schools (Robbins).

Writing club papers taught women skills and sharpened their minds. An article published in 1900 recounts, in humorous fashion, how members of a women's club worked collaboratively to find material for a paper on domestic servants (Anthony 30). The women described in this article learned to use Poole's Index and other library reference tools. For many women, reference tools were not the only unfamiliar aspect of preparing club papers; writing itself was foreign to them. As one nineteenth-century woman put it, club papers "gave us the habit of expressing ourselves on paper; they taught us not to fear the sound of our own voices" (Croly 59). Many women's clubs emulated college literary societies in appointing a critic who responded to papers presented. Like critics in college societies, holders of this office made suggestions for improvement. Where the office of critic was not used, club members relied upon more informal methods for responding to one another's papers, but, whatever the procedure, responses to papers contributed to women's development as writers.

A report from the Century Club of California explains the value of this development:

A glance at the committee work shows a large number of papers by women of the club. It will be seen that they furnished many of the most important scientific and literary essays; and the fact that the number of such papers increases year by year is the best proof of the power of women's clubs to educate and develop woman's ability. Such clubs are the instruments for broadening information on a vast number of topics, for teaching women to reason, for rendering their knowledge available, and for fitting them for the responsibilities of home as well as of public life. Perhaps one of the pleasantest features of these occasions is the pride evinced by all the members when a paper, denoting more than ordinary ability, is presented by one of their number. (Croly 251)

Some groups focused on writing exclusively or extended membership to writers only. The Scribblers of Buffalo, New York, for example, was formed in 1893 as "an organization of authors and newspaper writers" and, according to one of its members, had after three years left its "impress, even in this short while, on the press of Buffalo" (Croly 909). The Pacific Coast Women's Press Association, organized in California in 1890, did not limit its membership to newspaper writers but extended it to "any woman engaged in journalistic or literary work" (Croly 253). The New England Women's Press Association, a Boston group organized in 1885, limited membership to "any woman resident in New England who is connected as a professional writer, or manager, with any reputable newspaper or magazine" (Croly 641). Members of New York City's Heterodoxy (founded 1912) "wrote on a variety of subjects in various forms" (Schwarz 45).

Women's clubs, like college literary societies, preserved uneven records and sometimes lost them entirely. Even the names of all the clubs in a given community remain uncertain. Blair, for example, lists fourteen clubs active in Providence, Rhode Island, during the late nineteenth century but notes that her list is probably not exhaustive (67). My own archival research in Seattle unearthed more than twenty women's clubs. Some, such as the Seattle branch of the National Association of American Penwomen, were local chapters of national organizations. Many, however, were independent clubs initiated by women who shared social status, a common school or college, a neighborhood, a religion, or a profession. The roster of Seattle clubs included Classic Culture Club, Alpha, Nineteenth Century Literary Club, Apasia, Women's Century Club, Pennsylvania, Philomia, Sorosis, Cascadia, Chonian, Estella Bachman Brokaw Club, Women's Tuesday Club, Jefferson Park Ladies Improvement Club, Wednesday Evening Club, Queen Ann Fortnightly, Current Century, Women's Educational Club, DeCouvrir, Queen Anne Study Club, Episilon Sigma Alpha, Queen Anne Nomadic Circle, and the Pacific Improvement Club. Membership in these clubs varied from 12 to 200, but 20 was typical. Most of these clubs were organized between 1890 and 1915, and a few survive to the present, although many have disbanded.

While the majority of late-nineteenth-century self-improvement clubs were women's groups, there were some coed organizations as well as a few men's groups. Typical of these was the Seattle Writers

Club (founded 1903), which met weekly during its early years and had approximately 100 male and female members. Procedures varied from year to year, but the group always listened to approximately four selections by members at each meeting. In some years members were assigned specific dates for presenting manuscripts to the club, and in other years they proceeded more informally.

Minutes of meetings read like this one from July 14, 1914: "The program for the evening consisted of a story read by Mrs. Eastland and criticized by Mrs. Osborn. It was called 'The Suffragette Short Line.' All agreed that the plot was clever and new but many criticized the love making as gushy and lacking in picturesqueness and spice" (Potts). As this report suggests, critics were frequently assigned for specific meetings or pieces, but there was also opportunity for all present to respond. Occasionally general response was excessive, as suggested by this report from a meeting on October 25, 1910: "An attempt was made by certain members toward the suppression of free and unlimited speech on the part of the round table critics" (Potts). Excessive or not, participants in the Seattle Writers Club usually left meetings with a clear sense of the strong and weak points in their writing. The author of a story titled "Sealed Orders," for example, received this critique at the August 14, 1917, meeting: "On the positive side, it is interesting, there is some good characterization, the plot is out of the ordinary and therefore saleable, and young people would like it, but the opening is too slow, there are too many characters, it does not truly portray the character of American girls, some specific words and phrases don't work, and it is doubtful that there are any motor roads in the Black Forest."

Unlike some clubs, where members sought no audience beyond the immediate group, the Seattle Writer's Club gave considerable attention to publication by its members. Minutes of meetings include lists of authors who had recently had something accepted for publication, references to visits from publishers' representatives, and discussions of current publishing policies. One meeting, for example, gave time to protest The Ladies' Home Journal's recent keeping of 10,000 manuscripts submitted by participants in a writing contest instead of returning them or compensating the authors (Potts). At another meeting it is reported that a member "gave a report of her 12 years of writing, ending with September 1, 1916. Of 88 articles, 543,000 words, she has sold 49, for $1211.20. This makes an average of fifty six cents per hour for the time taken to write the 88 articles" (Potts). Considering that average workers' wages ranged between 25 and 40 cents an hour in 1916, this was not a bad return for her work (United States 164).

Ben Franklin's Junto began, then, a tradition stretching from 1728 to the present. Whether initiated to enlarge the intellectual sphere of young male clerks and apprentices or to liberate women from domestic isolation, the mutual improvement societies of this country nurtured the self-education of their members. By requiring members to write and share their work, mutual improvement societies functioned as writing groups, and they, like academic literary societies, contributed to the development of present-day writing groups. Today's groups, like their predecessors, encourage and enable individuals to improve their writing. In so doing they draw on the same impulses toward egalitarianism of knowledge and cooperative problem solving that have characterized Americans since colonial times.

Academic literary societies contributed directly to classroom writing groups, but the writing groups of mutual improvement societies exerted more subtle influences. As I have already noted, members of women's clubs often helped plan school curricula (Robbins), and their experience with self-sponsored writing groups no doubt led them to recommend similar procedures for students. Young men's mutual improvement societies likewise contributed to institutionalized education. Most notable were the mechanics' and workers' institutes that opened during the early nineteenth century. Typical of these, The Franklin Institute of Philadelphia stated its purpose as "the advancement of science and the mechanical arts, the increase of useful knowledge, the encouragement of invention and discovery, and the education of the public in the achievements of science and industry" (Nye 359). This and other institutes like it built upon the mutual improvement society concept by offering instruction at low cost with minimal enrollment requirements, and it included writing in "useful knowledge" to be increased.

Modern school-sponsored writing groups draw, indirectly at least, upon their nonacademic predecessors, just as they derive from college literary societies and writers' clubs. In today's schools and colleges, one manifestation of the connection between nonacademic writing groups and those in classrooms appears in Peter Elbow's

Writing without Teachers. As its title suggests, the book speaks to a population beyond the classroom, and its first lines address the self-improvement constituency: "Many people are now trying to become less helpless, both personally and politically: trying to claim more control over their own lives. One of the ways people most lack control over their own lives is through lacking control over words. Especially written words" (vii). Elbow explains that while he includes students in his audience, he is writing "especially [for] young people and adults not in school" (vii). The connection between nonacademic and school-sponsored writing groups becomes evident in Elbow's note to teachers. As he addresses teachers, Elbow argues that his method can be used in schools so long as teachers are willing to follow all the same procedures as everyone else, to put in their piece of writing each week, and get everyone's responses to it (ix). Elbow advocates, in other words, setting up a mutual improvement society in the classroom.

Elbow's suggestions make their way into classrooms through individuals, not by ways of large adoptions or curricular mandates. As he puts it, "the influence of the book worked more by having been read by individual teachers than by having been adopted in large numbers for classes" (letter). This implementation of Elbow's ideas in classrooms signals the connection between academic and non-academic writing groups.

Although men's and women's mutual improvement societies contributed to the writing groups that appear in today's schools, their more significant contribution was to the self-sponsored groups that continue to gather today. There is not, to be sure, a national umbrella such as the Chautauqua Literary and Science Circle or the Federation of Women's Clubs (although both still exist) under which all writing groups cluster, but individuals across the country gather in one another's homes, in churches, in cafes, and in municipal buildings to read and respond to one another's writing. The American tradition of egalitarian knowledge and cooperative problem solving continues to lead people to seek writing improvement through mutual improvement groups.

The noninstitutional nature of these self-sponsored writing groups makes it impossible to document numbers or even to estimate accurately how many such groups exist in this country today. Like the men's and women's organizations before them, these groups serve their members' needs, not those of researchers. My own anecdotal evidence indicates that archival records and publicly recognized organizations represent only a small percentage of the total number of self-sponsored writing groups. Through informal surveys I have learned about writers of retirement age who finally have the luxury of time, writers of special genres such as children's picture books or mysteries, writers of "serious" fiction and poetry—all of whom gather regularly to share and respond to writing in progress. Some of these groups have a stable membership while others change members frequently. And some are long-established groups while others have just formed; some give considerable attention to issues of publication while others simply share their work. The diversity of their configurations and the similarity of their concern with writing is matched by their relative invisibility, and more than once I have discovered accidentally that a long-time acquaintance has, without my knowing it, been a long-standing member of a writing group.

A more concrete indication of the extent of nonacademic writing groups appears in the marketing and sales of Peter Elbow's *Writing without Teachers*. As has already been discussed, both the title and the language of the introduction address individuals outside school, and the rest of the book continues to speak to this same population. Elbow talks directly to writers, making few references to schools and teachers. In particular, the two final chapters—"The Teacherless Writing Class" and "Thoughts on the Teacherless Writing Class"— inform persons who wish to establish their own writing groups. Elbow includes suggestions on qualities to seek in group members, procedures for running the "class," and difficulties to avoid. He also explains how he arrived at this approach and offers a rationale for its success. In other words, Elbow provides a "kit" for persons wishing to establish their own writing groups.

In recognition of Elbow's audience, the publisher of *Writing without Teachers* has marketed it as a trade book, not a text. As the proprietor of one bookstore explained, "It may be used as a text, but we sell it as a trade book." Purchasers, then, tend to be individuals who buy the book for their own use rather than because a class requires them to. When the book appeared in 1973 sales climbed to 10,000 a year, and they have remained steady at that level since. Because there have been only a handful of large adoptions over the years, and because the book is not marketed as a text, we can assume that a high percentage of the more than 100,000 owners of *Writing with-out Teachers* purchased the book to "become less helpless" about their writing, and a great many of them may have established their own writing groups. Although we cannot specify the exact degree, this kind of voluntary participation in writing groups builds upon the long-established tradition of mutual improvement societies in the United States and in so doing affirms the inherently social na-ture of writing.

Even when the academic and self-sponsored traditions of writing groups merge, as they do in Peter Elbow's book, they retain separate identities, because of the differing origins of authority in each type of group. In self-sponsored organizations, authority originates in in-dividual members who decide to join a group. As the history of these organizations reveals, individuals usually begin with some natural affinity of occupation (such as men employed as mechanics or women employed as journalists), of status (such as men whose socio-economic status foreclosed the possibility of higher education or women whose husband's occupation determined which of several clubs they joined), or of shared concerns (such as men interested in improving their skills or women interested in socially acceptable al-ternatives to domestic isolation). This affinity usually implies or leads to a mixture of friendship and good-will and respect among members. These shared positive feelings contribute to individuals' willingness to surrender their writing to the scrutiny and criticism of group members. In surrendering their writing, group members simultaneously give and accept authority. They give other individu-als the right to express reactions and make suggestions and with that giving of authority goes the implicit willingness to credit (at least in part) the responses of their peers with authority. Because authority originates in individual members rather than in something or some-one outside themselves, it always returns to them. They retain the right to leave the group, or to disregard the comments or advice of others.

Because authority resides ultimately in individual members of self-sponsored groups, the relationship among them is essentially nonhierarchical and gives more emphasis to cooperation than compe-tition. The "different voice" described by contemporary psychologist Carol Gilligan characterizes this relationship. Gilligan, in response to the disparity between women's experience and the dominant psychological representation of human development, offers an alternative view of development. As she puts it, "the different voice I describe is characterized not by gender but theme. Its association with women is an empirical observation. . . . But this association is not absolute, and the contrasts between male and female voices are presented here to highlight a distinction between two modes of thought . . . rather than to represent a generalization about either sex" (2). Gilligan's different voice emphasizes relationships over rules, connection over isolation, caring over violence, and a web of relationships over hierarchy. Self-sponsored writing groups incorporate this cluster of caring, connection, non-rule bound, nonhierarchical characteristics.

In school-sponsored groups, by contrast, authority originates in the instructor who directs students to share their writing with peers. Students thrust together in groups frequently begin with no affinity (although they may become friends as a result of their shared work), and often they have no say in choosing the participants in their group. They are simply given the common task of sharing and responding to writing. Furthermore, the grading system inherent in classes at all levels can lead group members to emphasize competition rather than cooperation. This competition is heightened when instructors employ more able students to monitor the work of their less able peers. Because group procedures are usually dictated by the instructor, participants may emphasize rules rather than relationships, and questions such as "What did she say we were supposed to do?" can figure prominently in student discussions. A hierarchical structure can result from the fact that authority originates in the institutionalized position of the instructor, one where individual participants look to the instructor rather than to one another for affirmation. This hierarchy undercuts the empowerment of individuals common in self-sponsored writing groups.

Despite their common potential for hierarchy, competition, and isolation, school-sponsored writing groups vary according to the amount of autonomy instructors allow them. Relatively autonomous groups develop when the instructor prepares students with models and guidelines for group standards and procedures and then allows groups to proceed largely on their own, interfering only for post-group evaluation. When instructors participate in and/or direct groups extensively, the groups gain no autonomy. In semi-autonomous groups students begin to take on authority to the extent that the instructor enables them to exercise it helpfully and responsibly. This means that students learn to emulate the giving and accepting of authority characteristic of self-sponsored groups. As they move away from positions articulated as "What right does another student have to comment on my paper" and "What right do I have to comment on another student's paper?" toward positions articulated as "I value the comments of my peers" and "My comments can help group members write better," classroom writing group participants become increasingly similar to their non-school counterparts.

Just as the influence of school-sponsored writing groups has been weakened by the intermingling of humanism, social meliorism, developmentalism, and social efficiency, so the differing sources of authority in self-sponsored and school-sponsored groups have contributed to their marginality. These different sources of authority account for the range from complete autonomy in self-sponsored groups to semi-autonomous and nonautonomous school-sponsored groups, and this difference in level of autonomy leads, in turn, to groups with vastly different characteristics, thereby diluting their effect. Writing groups have existed for more than two hundred years, but the continuing "discovery" of them demonstrates the extent to which they have remained on the edges of educational consciousness. Yet strength lies in that marginality because the periphery has the potential to renew whatever constitutes itself as the center. Writing groups of the literary society tradition enriched the college program so extensively that they were eventually incorporated into the curriculum. This process of incorporation began when courses offered by the University of Iowa's English department first included workshop procedures developed by Tabard and Ivy Lane, and it continues as individual instructors attempt to recreate their National Writing Project experiences for their students. Likewise, the center of mutual improvement societies shifted from young men's associations to Lyceum groups to Chautauqua circles to women's clubs to coed organizations, but writing groups, by remaining on the periphery, were able to add vitality to each. This vitality derives, in large measure, from investing writing with a social dimension, from demonstrating that writing is not an entirely isolated activity.

Part 2

Theory

3

Theories of Collaborative Learning

SHIFTING FROM A HISTORICAL ACCOUNT TO A THEORETICAL ONE means a change of degree, not kind. Just as history embodies theory, so theory draws on history, and the insights gleaned from looking at the origins and development of writing groups take on new dimensions when examined in the light of various theoretical perspectives. History, for example, reveals a recurring pattern of individuals gathering, either within or outside an institution, to improve their writing through mutual assistance. While history contextualizes some of the events and social forces surrounding this recurrence, theory expands upon historical context.

All writing group theory radiates from the fact that these groups assume a social definition of writing. But the term "social definition of writing," freighted with meaning, requires examination of sociological, political, philosophical, scientific, literary, rhetorical, linguistic, and psychological theory. A full exploration of all these theoretical dimensions lies beyond the scope of this work. Instead, I will concentrate on theories of collaborative learning and language development because these two incorporate a wide range of issues and center on pedagogical matters. Writing groups, both within and beyond academic institutions, exist as vehicles for learning, for helping individuals improve their writing. Accordingly, examination of their theoretical dimensions begins with their educational function.

Writing groups are generally catalogued under the heading "collaborative learning," a form of learning that includes a variety of learner-centered activities ranging from convening small groups to solve problems in a math class to organizing book groups that meet to discuss texts selected by members. The term itself may be a relatively new one. Kenneth Bruffee, for example, traces it back to Abercrombie's 1950s work with medical students at the University of London, work that demonstrated the superiority of collaborative learning over individual efforts for developing the medical judgment essential to diagnoses. When Abercrombie's medical students worked together they made much better diagnoses than when they worked individually. Bruffee also notes the 1960s contributions of Edwin Mason and Charity James to popularizing the term; both British secondary school teachers, they were committed to democratizing education and eliminating what they perceived as destructive social forms. Bruffee himself has also done a great deal to bring collaborative learning into the mainstream of academic discourse; the increased CCC and MLA attention he documents ("Collaborative Learning" 635) owes much to his work. But I think he is wrong when he writes that "the history of collaborative learning as I know it can be briefly sketched," reaching back only three decades for its origin ("Collaborative Learning" 636), because this statement conflates the term "collaborative learning" with the activities it describes.

Combining the two words "collaborative" and "learning" may be relatively new, but the work this term describes has, as chapters 1 and 2 demonstrate, a much longer history. Individuals who meet in writing groups to aid one another's learning participate in collaborative learning. The word "collaborative" suggests a perspective in opposition to the one usually associated with writers and writing. Most people think of writers as solo performers, individuals who isolate themselves from society to produce their work. This solo performer view permeates everyday conversational references to writers' garretts and real estate advertisements for "a writer's hideaway" or "secluded cottage ideal for writer."

It also dominates the politics of academic life. Most disciplines in the humanities emphasize individual perception, thus discouraging joint authorship; many pre-tenure professors are advised to avoid collaborative projects because they will not "count" in promotion and tenure reviews. Even established scholars encounter resistance to joint work. Sandra Gilbert and Susan Gubar, for example, report that they were encouraged to retain autonomy in their collaborative project, and in the preface to *The Madwoman in the Attic*, tucked between statements about the "exhilaration" of working together and claims that "the process of collaboration has given us the essential support we needed to complete such an ambitious project" (xiii), is a careful delineation of which chapters can be attributed to which author. Sandwiching assertions of individual accomplishment between approbations of joint work underlines the tension between the values of English studies and the Gilbert-Gubar collaboration.

Similarly, despite their quantity and variety, nearly all composition texts share an emphasis on individual effort in learning to write. They may be structured around the traditional modes of narration, description, exposition, and argument, or they may advocate a process approach to writing; but nearly all texts assume that writers learn and work alone. Texts such as Bruffee's *Short Course in Writing*, which advocate a group approach to writing, stand in sharp contrast to the vast majority that portray writing in individual, isolated terms. Text authors may exhort students to keep journals, to analyze their audiences, to re-vision their writing, or to recast their sentences, but they rarely mention working with others. Books by writing group advocates such as Elbow, Moffett, Macrorie, and Murray (see chapter 1) fall outside the text category. Indeed, claims for a paradigm shift in composition studies (Hairston) sound hollow in the face of the solo performer's continuing reign. The attention of theorists and researchers may have shifted from written product to the processes through which individuals produce writing, but this product/process dichotomy fails to address the social aspects of writing. The recently maligned "stage process" model of "prewrite, draft, revise," "recursive" variations on this model, and the complex diagrams of Flower and Hayes or Bereiter and Scardemalia all proceed from the assumption that writers work essentially alone.

Popular research methodologies reinforce the solo performer view of writing. Experimental design studies employing statistical analysis frequently look at interactions of features such as experimental treatment and writing performance, but interactions of writers are rarely included. Case studies focus on the experiences and behaviors of individual writers; readers of Janet Emig's *Composing Processes of Twelfth Graders* learned something about Lynn, who lived on "Pill Hill" in Chicago and wrote "Terpsichordean Greetings," but virtually nothing about her interactions with others, even though Lynn made very telling comments about her peers, comments I will discuss in chapter 4. Methodologies of composing aloud and protocol analysis both isolate writers—artificially according to some critics—to learn more about their cognitive processes during writing—again based on the assumption that writers' thoughts are entirely self-generated. Discourse-based interviews, which invite writers to comment on their own completed work, likewise assume that writing is an individual activity. There are, to be sure, exceptions. In recent years Lisa Ede and Andrea Lunsford have conducted research into collaborative writing and have employed surveys, interviews, and statistical analyses to learn about alternatives to solo performances in writing. And Karen Burke LeFevre's recent book argues that invention is a social, collaborative act, even when it is carried out by a single individual. But such studies stand outside the established tradition.

Despite its current dominance, the theoretical roots of this solo-performer view of writing lie in the relatively recent past. This view coincides with the eighteenth century legal-economic arguments and aesthetic perspectives that spawned "authorship," a concept Foucault describes as "the privileged moment of individualization in the history of ideas, knowledge, literature, philosophy and the sciences" (141). Up through the eighteenth century, writers were regarded either as artisans who manipulated traditional materials or, occasionally, as inspired beings who carried out the dictates of a muse. In the artisan role, writers were seen as knowing and employing the rules of rhetoric and poetics, and if their accomplishments extended beyond the artisan concept, they could be explained, as Milton did his own work, in terms of inspiration. In neither case was the writer considered personally responsible for written creations.

Accordingly, copyright law, when introduced in the sixteenth century, was designed to protect the rights of publishers, not writers. In 1533, for example, the Venetian senate granted printers "privileges" to print books, and in their early form these privileges allowed printing "without consent of authors or against their will" (Bowker 15). These privileges were not laws but dispensations giving individual printers exclusive rights to writing, which was otherwise considered public property. Because writers were viewed as either reassembling preexisting materials or following the directives of a muse, they could not claim ownership of what they produced. Once completed, writing moved into the public domain and could be used freely by anyone. Although it comes out of an entirely different context, this view bears remarkable similarity to one held by some contemporary literary critics. Jerome McGann, for example, insists that a literary text is "fundamentally social rather than personal" (8).

This pattern of governments granting printers (for a price) the right to publish—often without authors' consent and even against their will—extended throughout much of Europe and remained the dominant pattern for at least 200 years. Copyright was conceived as an economic transaction between printers and their governments, allowing printers the right to reproduce writing and sell it for profit. Writers, in the absence of any concept of intellectual property, could make little claim to what they produced and rarely received any remuneration from these transactions, relying instead upon patronage for their livelihoods.

During the eighteenth century, with its rapidly expanding population of readers, this situation changed as writers began trying to support themselves from the sale of their work. In England, the 1710 Statute of Anne changed the nature of copyright dramatically by placing the individual author at the center of protection. Although the speed with which it was adopted varied from one country to another, the Statute of Anne became the model on which subsequent copyright law was based. In the United States, for example, the first copyright legislation, enacted very shortly after the Revolutionary War, emulated the Statute of Anne directly. In Germany, where Martin Luther's view that knowledge received free from God should be freely given held sway, the concepts underlying the Statue of Anne took hold more slowly.

Because writers had to make a more convincing case for themselves in Germany, it was there, as Martha Woodmansee has demonstrated, that the modern concept of authorship was developed most fully. German resistance to the idea of writing as intellectual property took several forms, including the proposition that a book is not an ideal object but a real one that the author relinquishes in submitting a manuscript to a publisher and that, in different form, is subsequently sold to readers. According to this view, one remarkably similar to current reader-response theories, the pages covered with printed symbols do not contain ideas; these arise in the mind of readers. Even those who granted books more than physical qualities denied that ideas contained in a book could remain an author's property. In this view, once ideas have been expressed they cannot be called back and reclaimed by their originator any more than a preacher's sermon or a professor's lecture can be. Authors write for the express purpose of introducing their ideas into the larger community, and they cannot, therefore, seek to retain ownership of them.

Fichte's "Proof of the Illegality of Reprinting" (1793) drew upon the Englishman Edward Young's *Conjectures on Original Composition* (1759) to establish intellectual property rights for writers on the basis of originality of form. Acknowledging that neither the physical object nor the ideational content of the book could be claimed by the author, Fichte argued that because all individuals have their own way of thinking and forming ideas, one cannot appropriate another's ideas without altering their form. Accordingly, the form in which these ideas are presented remains "the property of the author eternally" (Woodmansee 445).

Edward Young, whose ideas of originality carried organic analogues, wrote out of a tradition more hospitable to the concept of authorship, with its attendant theories of originality and ownership. British religious traditions, little influenced by Luther's concept of free exchange of knowledge, posed no obstacle, and the seventeenth-century contributions of Hobbes and Locke opened the way for greater attention to individual writers. Hobbes, in taking a materialist view of the universe, lent authority to the emerging physics of his time. John Locke built upon this authority as he developed his theories of empiricism. Locke's insistence upon individual perception of sensory data combined with renewed attention to classical rhetoric's emphasis on the powers and activities of the rhetor, laying the groundwork for a developing interest in the writer's mind and the operation of that mind in writing.

This interest in the writer represented a departure from the long-standing aesthetic concern with audience, a concern M. H. Abrams describes as "the pragmatic orientation, ordering the aim of the artist and the character of the work to the nature, the needs, and the springs of pleasure in the audience, [which] characterized by far the greatest part of criticism from the time of Horace through the eighteenth century" (21). In declaring their departure from this long-standing emphasis upon the audience, writers of the romantic period spoke directly about the centrality of the writer's perceptions. Wordsworth, for example, described genius as "the introduction of a new element into the intellectual universe: or, if that be not allowed, it is the application of powers to objects on which they had not before been exercised, or the employment of them in such a manner as to produce effects hitherto unknown" (184). Achievement of this introduction depended upon an organic relationship between writers and their subjects, or what Robert Langbaum describes as "the subjective ground of commitment" (21).

Wordsworth and his contemporaries asserted that they, not established systems of thought, were central to knowing. It was not enough, in the romantic view, for writers to attain an objective understanding of their subjects. The romanticist, says Langbaum, projects "himself into the object, playing its role, knows himself in the object. . . . To know an object, the romanticist must be it" (25). This aesthetic concept of originality as genius interacted with the legal-economic concept of ownership, particularly as it was developed in Germany, to produce the modern concept of authorship

With the concept of authorship came a growing self-consciousness within writers, a growing attention to the relationships between one's own intellectual and emotional resources and the nature of the writing produced. What Foucault describes as the fundamental category of "the-man-and-his-work criticism" (141) emerged in response to this emphasis. Writers themselves responded by looking more closely at how they proceeded. Whether apocryphal, such as Coleridge's account of the inspiration leading to "Kubla Khan," or realistic, such as Wordsworth' explanation of the occasion and plan of "The Prelude," a new genre emerged—discourse in which writers discuss their own ways of writing.

This genre has flourished from the late eighteenth century to the present, as writers have become increasingly adept at discussing their own work. In 1957, for example, in introducing the first collection of *Paris Review Interviews*, Malcom Cowley could write: "The authors, more conscious of their craft than authors used to be, have talked about it with an engaging lack of stuffiness" (4). The consciousness spurring this collection and the self-consciousness enabling it both derive from the eighteenth-century emergence of the concept of authorship. And it was to accounts like these that Janet Emig turned when she first began exploring questions about writing processes.

By prefacing her study of twelfth-grade writers with published authors' discussions of their work, Emig called upon a long tradition of appropriating the concept of authorship for composition studies. Strictly speaking, the term "author," based on aesthetic and legal-economic theory, applies to a narrow range of publicly recognized discourse and does not include student writing. Composition students, after all, are not concerned with legal and economic rights to their work, nor is the question of individual genius a central one in most classes. The tradition of looking to expert models, however, has led composition studies to extend many of the attributes of authorship to student work. From its earliest days, composition instruction in this country has been based largely on emulation of authors' publications. Students were presented with exemplary selections from the works of noted writers and exhorted to do likewise. Not surprisingly, when emphasis shifted from product to process, the pattern of looking to experts reassembled itself to consider how authors wrote as well as what they wrote.

The solo-performer view of writing dominant in composition classes, then, owes much to the theory of authorship that emerged in the eighteenth century. This theory illuminates the opposition facing individuals who joined in collaborative efforts to improve writing. Not only were members of literary societies, young men's associations, and women's clubs thwarted by curricular limitations, humble circumstances, or the code of "ladydom," respectively, they also worked against the dominant theory of authorship. The symmetry between viewing writing as a solo performance and the prevailing theory of authorship was, however, matched by a subordinate pairing of collaborative practice and theory.

This subordinate pair of collaborative practice and theory has its roots in the late eighteenth century but was developed more fully in the nineteenth century. Although never as prominent as the aesthetic and legal-economic theories underlying the concept of authorship, theories supporting collaboration have an equally complicated history. The term alienation stands at their center. A complex and difficult term to define, alienation subsumes meanings including feelings of isolation, powerlessness, and meaninglessness. Early Scottish Enlightenment thinkers such as Adam Smith and Adam Ferguson identified alienation as one of the negative consequences of an industrial and laissez-faire economy, even though they approved of the economy in general. Ferguson, for example, warned that in a "commercial state . . . man is sometimes found a detached and solitary being" who deals with others "for the sake of the profits they bring" (122). British poets of the late eighteenth century voiced concern about the alienating quality of industrialization. Lines such as Wordsworth's "The World is too much with us; late and soon/Getting and spending, we lay waste our powers/Little we see in Nature that is ours" described technology's potential for isolating people from nature.

Nineteenth-century British writers such as Thomas Carlyle shared this anti-materialist view, arguing that industrialism loosed evil forces in the world, specifically those of alienation. He condemned a society in which "cash payment is . . . the sole nexus of man with man" because "love of men cannot be bought by cash-payment; and without love men cannot endure to be together" (174). Karl Marx echoed this view and went on to integrate it with Hegelian dialectics. Marx drew upon Hegel's distinction between humans as subjects and objects. For Hegel, this distinction focused on the dissociation between humans' creative attempts to realize themselves through what they produce and humans' capacity to be used or manipulated by others when their productions become alien objects. Hegel saw this as a philosophical distinction, but Marx framed it in political and economic terms, arguing that capitalism made workers into products by appropriating the products of their labor.

As Marx explained it in his *Economic and Philosophical Manuscripts of 1844*, the resulting alienation took three forms. First, workers are alienated from the objects of their labor because "the more the worker produces, the less he has to consume; the more values he creates, the less value, the less dignity, he has" (135). Second, workers are alienated from the act of production because labor does not belong to the essential being of the worker who "in his work, therefore, . . . does not affirm himself but denies himself, does not feel well but unhappy . . . feels himself only outside his work, and feels beside himself in his work. He is at home when he is not working, and when he is working he is not at home" (136). Third, workers are alienated from one another because workers confront one another as other workers. "What is true of man's relationship to his work, to the product of his work, and to himself, is also true of man's relationship to the other man, and to that man's labor and the object of his labor" (140–41). Marx saw the solution to this alienation not in terms of crude communism wherein envy leads to a leveling-down on the basis of a preconceived minimum. Rather, he urged a positive abolition of private property characterized by "the return of man himself as a *social*, i.e. really human, being" (149).

This insistence on humans' essentially social nature opposes alienation at the same time that it supports communal activities such as collaboration. Although Marxist theory has enjoyed a major role in discussions of eliminating alienation through emphasizing the social, communal aspects of human life, Marxism has not been the only source of theoretical support for collaboration in learning. Nineteenth-century sociologists such as Emile Durkheim and Ferdinand Tonnies concentrated on theories of "mass society," blaming industrialization for the loss of a sense of community. For theorists of mass society, this loss had many serious consequences, and the solution was to restore a sense of community among individuals. Durkheim, for example, wrote this about the importance of collaboration:

> When individual minds are not isolated but enter into close relation with and work upon each other, from their synthesis arises a new kind of psychic life. It is clearly distinguished by its peculiar intensity from that led by the solitary individual. . . . this activity is qualitatively different from the everyday life of the individual, as is the superior from the inferior, the ideal from the real. . . . periods of creation or renewal occur when men for various reasons are led into a closer relationship with each other, when reunions and assemblies are most frequent, relationships better maintained and the exchange of ideas most active. (91)

Durkheim's argument for collaboration underlines its creative power, suggesting the new capacities individuals find in themselves when they are freed from the alienation of isolation. This power of creativity helps explain the endurance of writing groups, explains why individuals have persisted, even when they found little social support, in gathering to participate in the "new kind of psychic life" available to them when they work with others. It also explains the sense of empowerment that so frequently accompanies writing group participation. Individuals feel empowered because they discover new capacities in themselves as they collaborate.

Concern with alienation extends into current literary theory, particularly in the Marxist school. Marxist critics reexamine the concept of authorship by describing writing in social terms. Raymond Williams, for example, argues that, because writing is a systematic skill that must be taught and learned, "the introduction of writing, and all the subsequent stages of its development, are intrinsically new forms of social relationship" (3). Williams goes on to claim that seeing writing and reading in social terms connects these activities inseparably with "the whole set of social practices and relationships which define writers and readers as active human beings, as distinct from the idealized and projected 'authors' and 'trained readers'" (189). In denying authors a privileged position Williams opens the door to extending the term to student writers.

Terry Eagleton assumes a similar stance when he castigates literary theory's "refusal to countenance social and historical realities" and its insistence upon "possessive individualism" or the belief that "at the centre of the world is the contemplative individual self, bowed over its book, striving to gain touch with experience, truth, reality, history or tradition" (196–97). Eagleton urges the alternative of rhetoric, because rhetoric sees writing and speaking as "forms of *activity* inseparable from the wider social relations between writers and readers, orators and audiences, and as largely unintelligible outside the social purposes and conditions in which they were embedded" (206). Not surprisingly, Eagleton sees signs of hope in mergings of cultural and political activity, and points with optimism to the emergence of British working-class writing. Eagleton describes members of this movement as breaking out of the "dominant relations of literary production" and "actively organizing to find their own literary styles and voices" (216).

The Republic of Letters describes the new genres, publishers, and forms of distribution of working-class writers, writers who aim to "disestablish literature, making writing a popular form of expression for all people rather than the preserve of a metropolitan or privileged elite" (Morley 1). Collaboration is central to these writers; they claim it as the source and exemplification of their energy, but at the same time they acknowledge the importance of solo-performance writing, asserting: "This dialectic between the individual as writer and as workshop member . . . lies behind many of the debates which continue to influence the direction of growth of the movement" (Morley 74).

Eagleton's enthusiasm for contemporary British working-class writing, a form of collaboration very similar to that of early American young men's associations or nineteenth-century women's clubs, demonstrates the consonance between his school of literary criticism and the collaborative impulse underlying writing groups. The enduring concept of alienation and the continuing struggle against it—a struggle that began with economists and poets of the eighteenth century, developed with Marxism and mass society theory, and continues in some schools of contemporary literary criticism— provides a theoretical foundation for collaboration. This foundation extends beyond contemporary Marxist critics. Jerome McGann, for example asserts that the final authority for literary texts "rests neither with the author nor with his affiliated institution; it resides in the actual structure of the agreements which these two cooperating authorities reach in specific cases" (54). McGann's insistence upon this fundamentally social existence for literary texts bespeaks his alignment with views of collaboration acted out in writing groups.

In pointing to rhetoric's potential for emphasizing the social relationships between writers and readers, Eagleton suggests the need to bring the two closer together. One of the benefits continually attributed to the collaboration of writing groups is that they bring writers and readers closer together, thereby providing writers a direct experience with audiences. Homer Watt, for example, writing in 1918, urged the use of writing groups because the scrutiny of their classmates would lead students to "real-author consciousness of an audience eager to challenge and to question" (160). Awareness of and responsiveness to audience constitutes one of writers' major problems.

If we conceptualize problem solving as including both the representation of a problem and the set of methods employed to solve it, writers face a wide range of problems extending from word to whole discourse level, and in every case they move through a number of possibilities before identifying a useful method. Finding the "right" word constitutes one sort of problem faced by writers, and reshaping a paragraph to address a given purpose or to develop an idea more fully constitutes another. Writing groups typically address this full range of problems, and they simultaneously deal with the overarching problem of audience awareness: overarching because a full range of writing problems emerges when writers do not or cannot consider their audiences.

Most theorists who discuss the problem of attending to audience in writing draw on the work of Jean Piaget. James Moffett, for example, claims that Piaget's concept of egocentricity can explain many writing problems. This inability to take another's perspective accounts for, says Moffett, "missing commas, poor transitions, 'faulty' logic, lack of focus, incoherence, anticlimax, and a host of traditional compositional problems" (57). Piaget's developmental theory suggests that problems of egocentricity should diminish as writers become older; nevertheless, as a number of researchers attest, inattention to audience persists well into adulthood, particularly among those designated as basic writers.

Mina Shaughnessy, who gave thoughtful attention to basic writers, concluded that egocentricity leads these writers to "the assumption that the reader understands what is going on in the writer's mind" (240). Andrea Lunsford describes basic writers as having "a consistent egocentricity, what Piaget calls 'centeredness,' in their writing" (3). The unskilled writers in Sondra Perl's study were portrayed as individuals who "wrote from an egocentric point of view. While they occasionally indicated a concern for their readers, they more often took the reader's understanding for granted. They did not see the necessity of making their referents explicit, of making the connections among their ideas apparent, of carefully and explicitly relating one phenomenon to another, or of placing narratives or generalizations within an orienting, conceptual framework" (332).

Elaine Maimon extends the egocentric definition to include all inexperienced writers, not just basic writers, noting that "the condition of the basic writer, like that of Piaget's young child, is a condition *in extremis* that we all share to some extent" (364). What we share is "egocentrism, in Piaget's sense of the word" (Maimon 364). None of these theorists offers a convincing justification for extending Piaget's "egocentrism" beyond the population of children it originally described, and, in my view, there is no such justification. Describing the problems of adult writers in terms of developmental psychology stretches the concept of "egocentrism" beyond the boundaries of its meaning and fails, finally, to address the essence of these problems.

A more fruitful explanation lies in the concept of alienation. Acknowledging that the dominant concept of authorship serves to isolate (and therefore frequently alienate) writers from their readers leads to the recognition that this alienation decreases writers' ability to visualize their audiences. If they perceive their work as removed from human interactions, writers are likely to feel isolated, particularly from their audiences. Accordingly, in their alienation, they will find it difficult to remember what their readers need to know and to find the right words to make their ideas most accessible to those readers.

Collaboration ameliorates alienation by reorienting writers toward their readers. Student writers in particular frequently undergo what John Trimble describes as a fundamental shift in their view of composing when they can conceptualize their readers. "The big breakthrough for the novice writer . . . will occur at the moment he begins to comprehend the social implications of what he's doing. Far from writing in a vacuum, he is conversing, in a very real sense, with another human being . . . even though that person . . . may be hours, or days, or even years away from him in time. This breakthrough is comparable to an infant's dawning realization that a world exists beyond himself" (15–16). Because it works against alienation, the collaboration of writing groups hastens that breakthrough. The peer who says "I don't understand" establishes—more powerfully than any theory, instructor's exhortation, or written comment can— the "otherness" of the audience and pushes writers to respond to this otherness by searching for more effective ways to convey ideas.

Also common among writers is alienation from the language to which they hold title. Students who slide their papers under the bottom of an instructor's stack may be merely self-conscious about their work, or they may actually be exhibiting a sense of alienation. Linguists such as William Labov have demonstrated that many speakers of English in the United States do not feel positive about the way they speak. I believe this linguistic self-hatred suggests that many writers may feel alienated from the language they use (Gere, "Public Opinion" 75–78). Collaboration in writing groups addresses this alienation by providing writers opportunities to explore the language of their linguistic community in the company of members of that community. Particularly in groups where oral readings occur, writers experience a new intimacy with their own words as they read aloud.

Collaboration that effectively reduces alienation appears in groups where no one individual constantly dominates, where all members are supported, and where individual contributions are developed upon by other members. The few extant records of meetings of young men's associations, literary societies, women's clubs, or classroom writing groups suggest that such collaboration was common in these groups. Indeed, complaints such as "To the LYFMOQS" found in Quadrangle's records testify to the common expectation that particular individuals or groups should not dominate. Although socioeconomic status and education may have created hierarchies both between and among women's clubs, organizational structures such as program planning and equitable distribution of requirements preserved collaboration.

Collaboration is a necessary but not sufficient condition for collaborative learning. While the democratic give-and-take of collaboration is essential, it does not by itself guarantee that any learning will take place. Participants in collaborative groups learn when they challenge one another with questions, when they use the evidence and information available to them, when they develop relationships among issues, when they evaluate their own thinking. In other words, they learn when they assume that knowledge is something they can help create rather than something to be received whole from someone else. An incipient form of this view appeared in what Boorstin describes as the colonial American assumption that "knowledge, like the New World itself, was still only half-discovered" (188). Boorstin's observation remains incipient because it portrays knowledge as an entity already existing in the world, waiting to be discovered. Had he used a phrase such as "half-created" or "half-generated," he would have captured the view of knowledge that underlies collaborative learning. This view of knowledge, variously described as social constructivist, antifoundational, and non-Cartesian, stands in opposition to more traditional views.

Just as the dominant view of authorship militated against a social perspective on writing until recently, so a fixed and hierarchical concept of knowledge worked against the idea of individuals striving together to create knowledge or to learn. The fixed concept derived from the view that knowledge resided in certain sources. From the middle ages until the eighteenth century, Saint Augustine's view of God as the source of knowledge reigned. In this view, the Bible, inspired by God, was the text from which knowledge could be extracted. As science gained ascendancy in the eighteenth century, mathematics eclipsed God as the ultimate source of knowledge. Although the source changed, the fixed view of knowledge prevailed. Those who sought knowledge had to immerse themselves in mathematics as they had once immersed themselves in biblical texts.

The hierarchical view, based on the idea that there is a special class of "knower," likewise shifted its focus but remained constant throughout the eighteenth century. When the Bible was perceived as the source of knowledge, the priests who studied scriptures identified and disseminated knowledge. For many years their monopoly on literacy, on copies of the Bible, and on knowledge of its original languages made impossible any challenge to their authority. Even though expanded literacy, the development of printing presses, and the translation of the Bible into vernacular languages diminished priests' exclusive hold on knowledge, the hierarchy they had established was simply transferred as scientists became the special class of "knowers."

Citizens of this country may have challenged the fixed and hierarchical view of knowledge with their literary society and club writing groups, but a major shift in perception of knowledge emerged, significantly, from science itself. From the seventeenth century until the twentieth the reigning view of science was built upon Descartes' division of the world into subjective mind and objective matter. Descartes assumed, in other words, that the mind could observe the universe but was not necessarily an interactive part of it. Newton subsequently adopted Descartes' mind-matter distinction, adding the independent existence of space and time. This meant visualizing the universe as a series of separate material objects, located in an invariant three-dimensional space, with time as a universal, separate dimension. In this view each material object had its own intrinsic properties, unmodified by environment. These concepts, the basis for classical physics, supported a fixed view of knowledge because they presumed that direct human perception of reality—unmediated, accurate, and separate in space—leads to a new understanding of the universe. Accuracy in predicting the paths of planets and similar successes helped confirm the validity of these concepts at the same time it solidified the prestige of trained scientists.

Because Cartesian-Newtonian physics provided such a useful model of the previously bewildering world of physical objects, it was soon transported to other fields and became part of the Western world view. Early psychologists, for example, adapted principles of classical physics to their investigations. Moreover, ideas of cause and effect, of the existence of separate objects with intrinsic properties, and of time and space as separate dimensions became part of accepted "common sense" ideas about the world. This adoption and acceptance helped foster the fixed and hierarchical view of knowledge.

But when Albert Einstein discovered in 1905 that the speed of light in a vacuum was always the same, even when measured by two different observers who were moving in relation to one another, classical physics could not provide an adequate explanation. Einstein was left to conclude that, contrary to Cartesian-Newtonian concepts, the physical dimensions and rate of time experienced by one observer must be seen as different from the point of view of the other observer. That is, time is not a separate, independent dimension but depends on the perspective of the observer. Einstein proposed that space, too, no longer be considered an independent dimension because the presence of matter distorts space. Einstein's work provided the first move toward abandoning a fixed view of knowledge by showing that observer and environment shape what we can know about our world.

Subsequent work in physics further invalidated fixed and hierarchical views of knowledge. Niels Bohr and Werner Heisenberg developed the principles of complementarity and indeterminacy that led to the development of quantum physics, an alternative to the Cartesian-Newtonian classical physics. With the recognition that a given entity can be categorized in more than one way, depending upon the circumstances under which it is observed and that the same objects of knowledge can have complementary properties that will exclude one another, came the beginning of a new view of knowledge, one less fixed and hierarchical. This shift did not take hold immediately in the social sciences, where physics had long provided the model for experimental design. Thomas Kuhn's *Structure of Scientific Revolutions* popularized this non-Cartesian alternative to classical physics, and in the years following its publication social scientists have increasingly reassessed the assumptions of their procedures. Kuhn's book undercut the Cartesian subjective/objective dichotomy by demonstrating that objectivity is a social construct, a function of the theoretical contexts within which researchers work.

Accordingly, in Kuhn's view, scientific knowledge is community property and science should be seen as a social activity in which disciplines develop their own rules of practice because observations are shaped by observers' preconceptions and circumstances.

The intellectual roots of a social definition of knowledge extend beyond science. The philosopher Richard Rorty draws on the work of Heidegger, Wittgenstein, and Dewey to construct his argument that "we understand knowledge when we understand the social justification of belief, and thus have no need to view it as accuracy of representation" (170). In Rorty's view knowledge emerges and is maintained in the "normal discourse" of communities of knowledgeable peers who tacitly agree to the same conventions and values. That is, they agree on a "set of conventions about what counts as a relevant contribution, what counts as a question, what counts as having a good argument for that answer or a good criticism of it." In so doing, they arrive at "the sort of statement that can be agreed to be true by all participants whom the other participants count as 'rational'" (320). Rorty thus extends Kuhn's argument that scientific knowledge is a social construct by claiming that all knowledge is socially generated.

Anthropologist Clifford Geertz takes a similar position, arguing that a social understanding of knowledge makes traditional general education impossible because the "enormous multiplicity of modern consciousness renders the image of a general orientation . . . shaping the direction of culture . . . a chimera" (161). His claim that our vocations are not "simply a trade we ply . . . [but] a world we inhabit" (161) echoes Kuhn's earlier statement about scientific communities, but its implications stretch much farther. For Geertz, all of life, in Java, Bali, Morocco, and in United States literature classes, enacts the mystery of "how it is that other people's creations can be so utterly their own and so deeply part of us" (54). The solution, according to Geertz, lies in "conceiving of cognition, emotion, motivation, perception, imagination, memory . . . whatever, as themselves, and directly, social affairs" (153). Although his specific cases focus on anthropologists, humanists (especially literary critics), and lawyers, Geertz, like Rorty, extends Kuhn's claims across all disciplinary lines.

Knowledge conceived as socially constructed or generated validates the "learning" part of collaborative learning because it assumes that the interactions of collaboration can lead to new knowledge or learning. A fixed and hierarchical view of knowledge, in contrast, assumes that learning can occur only when a designated "knower" imparts wisdom to those less well informed. Implicit in these two views of knowledge are two different definitions of language. Seen from the fixed and hierarchical perspective, language is a medium, the vehicle through which knowledge is transmitted. As such it remains on the margins of knowledge. The social constructivist view, by contrast places language at the center of knowledge because it constitutes the means by which ideas can be developed and explored. Kenneth Bruffee's discussion of collaborative learning underlines language's central role in developing ideas. Bruffee describes collaborative learning as providing a "community in which normal discourse occurs . . . a context in which students can practice and master the normal discourse exercised in established knowledge communities in the academic world and in business, government, and the professions" ("Conversation of Mankind" 642). Bruffee explains that students who are not members of the knowledge communities they hope to enter can help one another because no student is "wholly ignorant and inexperienced," because their conversation can be shaped by the teacher who is a member of that community, and, most importantly, because defining knowledge as socially derived means recognizing that taking a hand in the process of negotiating throughts, feelings, and perceptions constitutes learning.

Writing fits comfortably in the domain of collaborative learning because writing demands dialogue between writer and context. Writing can succeed only when it adheres to the conventions of "normal discourse" for a given community, and writers can learn this discourse through using it in the kinds of conversations that occur in collaborative learning. The varieties of "normal discourse" are evident in the many types and styles that fall under the category of "good writing." Differences in circumstances of audience and purpose determine how writing is perceived. Prose effective for an editorial in a small town newspaper would not serve for, say, a column in *The New Yorker*. Quality assessments of writing reflect a continuing negotiation between writers and their social contexts.

Examination of the language of writing groups reveals that negotiation, rather than application of absolute standards, guides participants as they aid one another toward better drafts (Gere and Stevens). The language is often tentative, with phrases such as "I don't know" or "I don't think" occurring frequently. Participants frame comments in terms of their own experience with the writing rather than some "ideal" text, and in so doing they avoid standardized comments that can be transposed from one piece of writing to another. Particularly in established groups, writers begin to comment on or ask questions about their own work. They say things such as: "I don't know whether this sentence belongs here"; "Will it look bad if I use the quote she used?"; and "Usually I write everything I can think of first and then cut it down later. What do you do?" These participants involve others directly in the forms and processes of their own writing. They also use the group as a place to explore their goals ("I want to show why Joe came to be so alienated from his family"), to find promising directions ("Why don't you put the part about the house later so it doesn't get in the way of the explanation?"), and to make relationships between ideas more explicit ("The war started because of the selfishness of a few men. Do you think that's how war starts? I mean sometimes people say that but . . . people don't have to support it. . . . war is caused by a clash between people, between groups of people. I mean it didn't start by, you know, a few men getting together"). Such negotiations demonstrate the capacity of writing group participants to work together in creating knowledge.

This social process of developing knowledge about writing enables writers to transform their unfinished or indeterminate texts into more finished form. The language through which writing group participants accomplish this transformation falls into what James Kinneavy, drawing on the work of John Dewey, calls exploratory language. Kinneavy describes exploratory discourse as leading to changes in intellectual views (100). It is frequently oral and dialectic rather than rigidly controlled by an objective reality. Ambiguity is important to exploratory discourse because "the nature of the reference may still be in question and to impose a one-to-one relation of language to reality might be to close the door to possible real meaning(s) the word may have" (189).

Kinneavy's description of exploratory language draws on what John Dewey calls "a pattern of Inquiry," or controlled transformation of an indeterminate situation into a determinate one (104–5). The unfinished text constitutes the indeterminate situation in the

writing group, and the importance of this indeterminacy appears
most clearly when such a text is not present. Gere and Stevens, for
example, found that when participants in writing groups read "finished" writing, the language of the group often became acerbic or
vacuous because members felt (perhaps unconsciously) that they
had no purpose.

When the text is perceived as unfinished or indeterminate, the
writing group provides a forum in which writers "learn" how to
make it more finished. This process of learning about particular
texts illustrates the importance of a social definition of knowledge.
The textual indeterminacy essential to writing groups is, of course,
integral to writing itself. Writing rarely proceeds by way of a single
text, and most finished (or abandoned) texts consist of layers of previous or "shadow" texts, as Louise Weatherbee Phelps calls them.
The strata of shadow texts underlying a finished text often remain
invisible to inexperienced readers and writers and, when reinforced
by the notions of individual ideas inherent in the solo-performer
view of authorship, lead to a truncated perception of what it means
to write. The social view of knowledge, which assumes an indeterminate text in writing groups, supports an enriched concept of
writing.

Theories of collaborative learning, then, build upon an opposition to alienation and to the highly individualistic view inherent in
traditional concepts of authorship and emphasize the communal aspects of intellectual life. In the collaborative view individual genius
becomes subordinate to social interactions and intellectual negotiations among peers. When writing constitutes the task of collaboration, the process of working together enables writers to use language as a means of becoming competent in the discourse of a given
community. *Learning*, when conceived in collaborative terms, assumes a socially derived view of knowledge and opposes a fixed and
hierarchical one. The exploratory discourse of writing groups demonstrates the capacity of these groups to develop knowledge about
the texts under consideration.

These texts, indeterminate, unfinished, occupy the center of
writing groups, uniting theories of collaboration and learning. Like
light, which can be seen as both particles and waves, these texts are
subject to multiple interpretations and suggestions from group participants. This exploratory process helps transform indeterminmate

texts into more determinate or finished ones while at the same time enabling participants to experience the indeterminacy inherent in the shadow texts of writing. Although individual writers still retain ultimate responsibility for their texts, processes of collaboration underline the social dimensions of writing.

Seeing collaborative learning from the perspective of a social view of knowledge reveals a conceptual obstacle that has dogged writing groups throughout their history. Writing groups have consistently operated within a Cartesian framework where language serves as the medium for conveying (rather than developing) ideas. James Moffett's work exemplifies the problem inherent in the Cartesian perspective. Moffett begins from the premise that "dialogue is the major means of developing thought and language" (73) and goes on to claim that learning to use language "requires the particular feedback of human response" (191), urging that students "write for each other" (193). Yet Moffett goes on to claim that writing means "going it alone" (87). The gap between Moffett's statements about language learning and his insistence on writing as an isolated activity derive from the Cartesian dichotomy between the individual and society.

Although his statements about dialogue suggest a social view, Moffett retreats from this position to stay within the Cartesian perspective that separates from society the individual writer who is "going it alone." In so retreating, Moffett takes the inconsistent position of claiming that language can at one moment function socially, generating knowledge, and at another moment become the conduit through which an isolated individual conveys ideas. Like many other advocates, past and present, Moffett confronts conceptual obstacles to reconciling writing groups with Cartesian epistemology. The dissonance between Cartesian epistemology and writing groups accounts for much of the marginality of writing groups across time because writing groups were repeatedly thrust into an intellectual environment unable to support them. Thus theory helps explain history.

4

Theories of Language Development

IN FOCUSING ON THE IMPROVEMENT OF WRITING, WRITING GROUPS
are, ultimately, concerned with language development. Individuals
join and participate in these groups because they (on their own or at
an instructor's insistence) wish to write better, and their improvement depends upon developing greater fluency with language. Accordingly, this chapter considers theories of language development
in relation to the linguistic transactions of writing groups.

The most widely accepted theory of language development derives from the work of developmental psychologist Jean Piaget. In
his description of maturation, Piaget emphasizes the individual's
transition from egocentrism (which puts the self at the center) to a
more decentered perspective (which enables one to see from other's
viewpoints). Although Piaget's theory assumes that the process of
development is aided by socialization, it assigns an asocial genesis to
egocentric speech. In other words, encounters with others help individuals develop decentered language, but egocentric speech originates within the individual, not from social interaction.

Piagetian theory emerges from Cartesian epistemology, as demonstrated by its separation of individual and society, its description
of development as a hierarchical progression, its focus on the nature
of individual thought, and its characterization of knowledge as a
fixed entity. Piaget accepted, as have most Westerners, the mind-
matter division and applied Cartesian rationalism to describing the
mind's development. Not surprisingly, the tradition of cognitive psychology that built upon Piaget's work is likewise Cartesian in its description of individuals' ways of knowing.

The Piagetian view portrays writing as a fundamentally individual

activity. Language, which begins within the individual, must ultimately reside there; the challenge of writing is to become less de-
pendent upon others. James Moffett, one of the first composition
theorists to draw on Piaget's work, describes learning to write in
highly individualistic terms: "To ask a student to write is to ask him
to make all the adjustments between dialogue and monologue that I
have been describing. . . . The most critical adjustment one makes
is to relinquish collaborative discourse, with its reciprocal prompt-
ing and cognitive co-operation, and to go it alone" (87).

Other theorists also see learning to write as a process of relin-
quishing collaborative discourse and going it alone. Janet Emig, who
is generally credited with popularizing the term "composing processes," conceptualized writing in individual terms. Her description of writing as a solo performance derives from Piaget's asocial
model of language development, and this model, in turn, results
from the Cartesian epistemology in which Piaget's work is framed.
Emig's Cartesian perspective is evident in her method of asking isolated students to compose aloud and her concentration upon their
individual perceptions and experiences. Emig values information
about her subjects' families, living situations, schools, and teachers
to the extent that it contributes to the individual psyche under consideration. This concentration upon individual writers comes at the
expense of societal factors, even though evidence of these factors
appears throughout Emig's study.

Lynn, the student to whom Emig gives most attention, makes a
number of evocative comments about her peers: "I've always had
trouble talking to people about my feelings on something. . . . I can
talk about facts more easily than I can talk about abstract things . . .
when . . . I was at this Institute, one of the kids kept saying, 'Lynn,
you know, you're a great kid but you know it doesn't come out in our
discussion group because you seem to be talking in cliches, you
never seem to be talking about yourself, about your own feelings,
you seem to be giving examples,' I don't know why this is" (49). In
saying this Lynn indicates that interactions with her peers have
shaped her perceptions of herself as a writer, helping her to see
areas of strength and weakness. Later she says: "This one girl in our
class . . . was getting B's again instead of A's although I thought her
writing was much better than most of the kids in our class" (70) and
"I'm always afraid of being too corny because there are some kids in

my class who write like that" (72). Both statements demonstrate how Lynn's peers have contributed to her understanding of quality in writing, and all three comments suggest a rich network of social interactions that contribute to Lynn's writing processes. Yet, within the Cartesian, author-centered framework in which her study is cast, Emig does not—cannot—give them more than passing attention. Although Emig's description of writing processes spurred much enlightened teaching and considerable research, it also furthered an author-centered view of writing, one consonant with the solo-performer concept.

Implicit in this author-centered view of writing is an inside-outside delineation, corresponding to Piaget's view of egocentric language. Writing is conceived as originating within the author and then being externalized in written form. This conception dichotomizes individual writers and their social contexts. Emig's description of reflexive and extensive modes manifests this division. According to Emig, the reflexive mode "focuses upon the writer's thoughts and feelings concerning his experiences; the chief audience is the writer himself" (4), while the extensive mode "focuses upon the writer's conveying a message or a communication to another" (4). Although all mean slightly different things, formulations such as James Britton's expressive-transactional functions and Linda Flower's writer-based and reader-based prose share Emig's emphasis on separating the writer and society. Likewise, Britton and Flower both propose models of composing that focus exclusively on the individual writer.

Conceptualizations such as Moffett's, Emig's, Britton's, and Flower's—because their foundations lie in Piaget's asocial concept of language development and in traditional epistemology—dichotomize writing into dialogue/monologue, society/individual, inner/outer, thereby creating oppositions rather than complementarities. So long as writing is conceived in dichotomous terms, the interaction of individual and society, of dialogue and monologue, and of internal and external remains impossible within Cartesian epistemological metaphors. Fred Newton Scott long ago recognized the problem with this separation. In his "English Composition as a Mode of Behavior," Scott describes errors in writing as symptoms of an "inward disease" (463) and cites as the cause "the clash between, on the one hand, the instinctive, inherited impulse to communication, and, on the other hand, the scholastic system of abstract symbolism which, under the name of language studies, grammar, and rhetoric, we now use in the schools and regard as an indispensable medium of culture" (467). Implicit in the clash Scott describes are the terms *individual* and *social*. Operating as he does within a Cartesian epistemology, Scott urges the solution of "bringing the dissociated things together" (29), thereby suggesting a bridge between individual and society. Such bridge terms are, as Rorty notes, characteristic of Cartesian thought, but creating a bridge does not change the nature of the individual-society dichotomy. Thus, the union Scott urges remains impossible in the epistemological tradition within which he operates.

A clear manifestation of the Cartesian epistemology within which the Piagetian model lies is the metaphors it generates. Specifically, Piaget's theories generate a locked internal box metaphor for writers. According to this perspective writers are people who open the lids of their minds to gain access to what is locked inside. Much of the language of composition studies reflects the power of this metaphor. Terms such as *brainstorming* and *getting it out* imply the need to release language stored inside the writer, while words such as *writer's block* and *stopping the flow* connote the difficulty of con-·tinuing access to the mind's inner chambers. In her examination of metaphorical language used by writers to describe their processes, Barbara Tomlinson cites authors who appropriate the language of mining as they talk about poems leading a "buried life in the mind" (Stanley Kunitz) or realizing "a poem is buried there" (Anne Sexton) or working "from some deep down place" (Henry Miller). Such metaphors represent writing as a difficult process of extracting material, thereby reinforcing the idea of the mind as a closed box and of language as nothing more than a conduit connecting internal and external worlds. Frequently, because it fits so well with Cartesian dichotomies, this metaphor overshadows all other formulations, or as John Trimbur has noted, "one current in the cultural development of consciousness [is made into] a natural law" (7). The inherent problem of such broad acceptance lies in its potential to overwhelm all other interpretations, creating a sea of Cartesian epistemology in which the water becomes invisible to those swimming in it.

Alternative views lie close at hand if one can see them. Stephen Toulmin's distinction between interiority and inwardness, for example, demonstrates the fallacy of describing inner speech in such narrow terms. Interiority, according to Toulmin, is dictated by our physiological nature, while inwardness is learned. Because of the location of our brains, we cannot help feeling that verbal thought occurs in the interior of our heads, but the inwardness of mental life is acquired through cultural experience and human development. We make reading, for example, an inward experience as we learn to read silently rather than aloud, but reading is not inherently an interior experience. Oral reading is always possible and was, for a long period in history, the dominant form. Accordingly, says Toulmin, we should avoid "confusing the neurological processes with the inwardness of mental experience" (8). In other words, while it is physiologically necessary to conceive of inner speech as occurring inside our heads, it does not follow that it must be an entirely inward mental experience. So, too, physiology dictates that some parts of writing occur in writers' minds, but not all of it need be inward. Yet this is the conclusion implicit in applying Piaget's Cartesian model of language development to writing.

Less well known than Piaget's is Vygotsky's theory of language development, and it assumes a social genesis for language. Vygotsky shares Piaget's perception that inner speech constitutes one of the stages of language development, but he disagrees fundamentally about its nature. For Vygotsky the source of language lies outside the individual, and instead of being a transition from asocial to social language, egocentric or inner speech is a continuation of socially and environmentally oriented language development. Like Piaget, Vygotsky documented his pronouncements with experimentation, specifically by removing the possibility for social interaction by isolating children, putting them in rooms with deaf mutes, or playing very loud music. Because egocentric speech decreased dramatically in these situations, Vygotsky concluded that this language was indeed social in nature and claimed, "Development in thinking is not from the individual to the socialized, but from the social to the individual" (*Thought and Language* 20). In Vygotsky's view, language follows a similar pattern of development; its origins are social: "Egocentric speech emerges," Vygotsky claims, "when the child transfers social, collaborative forms of behavior to the sphere of inner-personal functions" (*Thought and Language* 19). This transfer does not, however, isolate individual and social language; they remain interlocked because individual language is internalized social language.

An illustration of the continuing connection between individual and social language appears in Vygotsky's delineation of sense and meaning in words:

> The sense of a word . . . is the sum of all the psychological events aroused in our consciousness by the word. . . . Meaning is only one of the zones of sense, the most stable and precise zone. A word acquires its sense from the context in which it appears; in different contexts, it changes its sense. Meaning remains stable throughout the changes of sense. The dictionary meaning of a word is no more than a stone in the edifice of sense, no more than a potentiality that finds diversified realization in speech. (*Thought and Language* 146)

Thus, the dictionary meaning an individual carries around interacts, then, with its social context to create the sense of the word. The word "nice," for instance, can indicate praise in one context and sarcastic reprimand in another. What Vygotsky describes as the "complex, mobile" sense of the word (*Thought and Language* 146) derives from this interaction or dialectic between the individual and society. Inner speech may compress social interchanges into abbreviated and individualistic verbal thought, but this language still maintains the relationship of the individual to the social environment.

Recent research substantiates Vygotsky's claims for the social genesis of language. John and Goldstein, for example, found that children develop and test their tentative ideas about meaning and form "chiefly through verbal interaction with more verbally mature speakers" (266). Smith and Miller examined parent-infant collaboration to discern its contribution to children's understanding of the significant differences and regularities of language, and they concluded that this collaboration creates the foundation for subsequent language development.

Other research with young children reinforces this claim for the social genesis of language. Trevarthen and Hubley observed turn-taking in infants of three to four months and found that by four to six months infants follow their parents' gaze (Bruner). Before they are a year old, children bring things to their parents' attention by presenting them or pointing to them. Condon and Sander claim that social interaction may be present from birth because one-day-old infants synchronize their movements to segments of human speech. Before infants are two months old, their parents attribute intention to their gestures, thus reinforcing the social dimension of the infants' behavior (Stern 189). All of these prelinguistic forms of communication reinforce the validity of seeing the origins of language development in society rather than within the individual. Yet, in Vygotsky's terms, acknowledging the social derivation of language does not obviate the dialectic between it and inner language.

Dialectic occurs because the process of internalization is not a simple matter of copying something external. Rather it involves the formation of an internal "plane of consciousness" (Wertsch 64). Internalization, as Vygotsky sees it, bears a close relationship to the social origins of individual psychological processes, particularly higher level mental functions. These functions appear initially in the external world because they are social processes: "It is necessary that everything internal in higher forms was external, that is, for others it was what it now is for oneself. Any higher mental function necessarily goes through an external stage in its development because it is initially a social function" (Wertsch 62).

Vygotsky terms the region where this transition from social to individual or interpsychological to intrapsychological occurs as the *zone of proximal development* which he defines as "the distance between the actual developmental level as determined by independent problem solving and the level of potential development as determined through problem solving under adult guidance or in collaboration with more capable peers" and incorporates "those functions that have not matured but are in the process of maturation. . . . the 'buds' or 'flowers' . . . rather than the 'fruits' of development (*Mind in Society* 86). For Vygotsky internalization depends not upon large societal processes but upon what Wertsch describes as "small groups . . . of individuals engaged in concrete social interaction . . . explainable in terms of small group dynamics and communicative practices" (60). Social interactions that aid the process of internalization, then, include those of writing groups.

Indeed, Vygotsky's perspective on the dialectic between individual and society has much more congruence with the activities of writing groups than does Piaget's Cartesian, dichotomous view. In Piagetian terms, writing groups provide a means to the end of individual performance in writing, but they are finally peripheral because the essence of writing lies in the individual effort of opening the mind's locked lid. Vygotsky's insistence on the dialectic between the individual and society, however, puts peer response at the center of writing because it makes language integral to thinking and knowing. The generative qualities Vygotsky attributes to language underline his social view of knowledge.

Some contemporary composition theorists have incorporated Vygotsky's views. Kenneth Bruffee, long an advocate of writing groups, explains the dialectic of speaking and writing: "If thought is internalized public and social talk, then writing of all kinds is internalized social talk made public and social again. If thought is internal conversation, then writing is internal conversation re-externalized. . . . Writing is at once both two steps away from conversation and a return to conversation. We converse; we internalize conversation as a thought; and then by writing we re-immerse conversation in its extensive social medium" ("Conversation of Mankind" 641).

The voices students hear in writing groups contribute directly to what they internalize and later use in writing. Without the opportunity to participate in the dialogue of writing groups, students have one less chance to converse with the society around them. Throughout the years, from 1880 forward, commentators have noted the positive feelings that accompany participation in writing groups (see Lord; Bibliography). Motivation toward writing increases, anxiety about writing decreases, and writers develop feelings of trust and community. Writing groups generate these positive feelings because they provide writers with a language in which to talk about the writing problems they encounter, and thus a tool for solving them. This language about language becomes part of what Vygotsky calls the interpsychological process, another way for writers to participate in conversation with the community they are in the process of joining.

A key benefit of this conversation within writing groups, as opposed to the individual experience of other approaches to writing, is that it blurs the distinction between writer and audience. Writing group participants become both writer and audience, incorporating the "otherness" of the audience into their own writing. In the process, both writers and audience become members of the same language community; they learn to speak the same vernacular. This process is similar to what Stanley Fish describes as the development of an interpretive community of readers. For Fish, "there is no single way of reading that is correct or natural, only 'ways of reading' that are extensions of community perspectives" (16), and these ways evolve from changing interpretive communities. For Fish, of course, the interpretive community consists of literary critics and their students, but for writers, peer response creates an interpretive community with which the writer can maintain a Vygotskian dialogue throughout the process of writing.

The obvious value of Vygotsky's formulations makes their relative obscurity puzzling. For some time, political barriers prevented dissemination and acceptance of Vygotsky's work in this country. *Thought and Language* was first issued in 1934, but the Russian government suppressed it in 1936, and it did not reappear until 1956. The book has been readily available in the United States since 1962 and has received increased attention in recent years. Evidence of Vygotsky's growing prominence lies in the 1978 publication of a collection of his essays (*Mind in Society*), but a substantial portion of his work remains unavailable to Western readers. More powerful than the political obstacles to Vygotsky's work were the intellectual ones founded in Cartesian epistemology but taking specific form in language study. These obstacles contributed to the marginality of writing groups.

Vygotsky, along with his contemporary Mikhail Bakhtin, represents a radical departure from the received tradition of language study in this country. Ferdinand de Saussure's opposition of *langue/ parole*, synchronic/diachronic, and syntagmatic/paradigmatic during the early years of this century had a powerful influence on the shape of American linguistics up to and including Noam Chomsky's competence/performance distinction. In particular Saussure's distinction between *langue*, or the collection of social conventions that enables individuals to communicate in a given community, and *parole*, or the individual's combination that creates a message, became institutionalized as a central tenet of linguistics. Saussure made his intention explicit by asserting that his approach permitted a separation of "what is social from what is individual" (14). By insisting that an individual's language and that available in the surrounding community are different in type, Saussure separated internal and external language. As a result, he argued, study of internal and external language requires different methods: "External linguistics can add detail to detail without being caught in the vise of a system. . . . In internal linguistics the picture differs completely. Just any arrangements will not do. Language is a system that has its own arrangement" (22). This description of language reflects the dichotomies of Cartesian epistemology.

Piaget's separation of inner and external speech fit comfortably within Saussure's intellectual milieu. Piaget's work was also compatible with Sigmund Freud's concept of the individual psyche. The description of children moving from the "pleasure" of autistic thought to the "reality" imposed by society paralleled Freud's pleasure principle and reality principle. In addition, Piaget and Freud shared an interest in looking at the individual in isolation rather than in social terms. Neither Freud's individualistic subjectivism nor Saussure's oppositions was, however, accepted by intellectuals in the Soviet Union in the 1920s. Vygotsky's insistence on the interrelationship between adult social speech and inner language demonstrates his opposition to dividing the individual and society. Although there is no evidence that Vygotsky and his contemporary Mikhail Bakhtin were familiar with one another's work, they, like other Soviet intellectuals of the early part of this century, shared an interest in countering Freud's individualism and restructuring the Saussurean dichotomy by demonstrating an integration between the individual and society. This interest was consonant with but not limited by Marxist social theory. Vygotsky's interest in accounting for the relationship between society and human consciousness clearly followed Marxist lines, but his research never extended beyond the interpsychological level of small groups of individuals discussing concrete problems.

Vygotsky made his contribution in the area of psychology while Bakhtin was primarily a literary critic. Yet Bakhtin's contributions included a radical redefinition of the psyche as a social entity. In *Marxism and the Philosophy of Language*, a book listed as authored by V. N. Volosinov but generally credited to Bakhtin (Emerson 263), he writes that the psyche "enjoys extraterritorial status . . . [as] a social entity that penetrates inside the organism of the individual person" (39). To arrive at this position, Bakhtin posits four social factors: First, the word and its effects occur in outer (rather than internal) experience. Second, this outer experience is in some way organized socially. Third, idea systems exist as a relation between speakers and listeners or between social groups; because no two individuals ever share exactly the same experiences or belong to precisely the same social groups, speakers and listeners and writers and readers constantly translate and negotiate meanings interactively. And fourth, words do not come from dictionaries but from dialogue.

Bakhtin's fourth social premise shares much with Vygotsky's distinction between meaning and sense. For both of them "meaning" refers to the dictionary definition of words, and Vygotsky's term "sense" resembles Bakhtin's term "theme." In Bakhtin's terms, words cannot be separated from their speakers, and as they occur in dialogue they are invested with "theme." He defines theme this way: "Theme is the *Upper, Actual Limit of Linguistic Significance*; in essence, only theme means something definite. Meaning is the *Lower Limit* of linguistic significance. Meaning, in essence, means nothing; it only possesses potentiality—the possibility of having a meaning within a concrete theme" (101). The similarity between Vygotsky's and Bakhtin's formulations demonstrates that Vygotsky was not working in isolation but was part of a larger intellectual community, one quite unlike that in the West.

Considering Vygotsky's intellectual context helps explain why his work has taken so long to receive attention in this country, and, indirectly, why writing groups remained for so long on the margins of the curriculum. The Cartesian-based individualistic aspect of Freud, Saussurean dichotomies, and asocial Piagetian principles that made Vygotsky's work difficult to assimilate also contributed to the peripheral nature of writing groups. Led to writing groups chiefly by the pressures of too many students and/or too many papers, instructors often went on to to ascribe value to the audience awareness they engendered. But this value, because it was framed in Piagetian terms, took provisional form. If one sees the ability to "go it alone" as the goal of writing, then the interaction of writing groups must ultimately, along with all other forms of dialogue, be abandoned. From the Vygotsky/Bakhtin perspective, however, peer response plays an essential part in writing because this exchange contributes to the continuing dialogue between individual writers and their society.

If we accept the idea that language is socially constituted and that the "sense" of words (as Vygotsky uses the term) emerges from the context in which they are used, then dialogue becomes more than a preliminary to writing; it is essential to the whole activity: essential because the language writers use depends upon their social participation, and peer response provides a specialized society for writers. The process of being exposed to the work of others and of engaging in discussions about one's own writing provides writers a unique opportunity to engage in the society of other writers. It is this society, a society integral to the essence of writing, not a stepping stone toward a solo performance, that contributes to the language development inherent in writing groups.

In this society, writers do more than offer one another helpful advice; they exchange meanings. As Bakhtin puts it, "As a living, socio-ideological concrete thing, as heteroglot opinion, language, for the individual consciousness, lies on the borderline between oneself and the other. The word in language is half someone else's" (*Dialogic Imagination* 293). The dialogue of peer response, then, gives life to Bakhtin's claim that words are always half someone else's by putting writers in a context where they create language as part of their dialogue with others.

Here, for example, is an excerpt from a writing group's discussion of an essay on *The Red Badge Of Courage*. This excerpt is part of the data collected for an empirical study (Gere and Abbott) of the language of writing groups.

Danny, one of the participants, reads a summary statement from his essay:

Danny: All through *The Red Badge of Courage*, Henry tries to become a man, and when he finally does, he finds it is not what he expected.
Tom: Do you think that was what he trying to do though?
Danny: Yeah.
Tom: Do you?
Sarah: I don't think . . .
Danny: Of course . . .
Sarah: I don't think he set out with that purpose in mind.
Danny: No.
Tom: To say "I'm going to be a man."

Danny: "No, but he is just kind of trying to prove himself to be able to say, "I'm a man," well you know.

Sarah: I . . . I got the idea he . . .

Tom: He may have felt this way when he made it through a battle.

Sarah: Yeah, and like he, he was saying he wanted stories to tell his kids.

Tom: Yeah.

Danny: OK.

Sarah: That sort of deal. He wanted to be a hero. He wanted to be looked up to.

Tom: Yeah, he wanted to be a hero, that's what it was.

Danny: Oh, so Henry tries to be a hero when he finally becomes a . . . OK, can I see your pencil?

Tom: Sure.

Danny: Thanks.

Sarah: So what are you going to use to back it up?

Danny: Well, there . . . I am going to talk about first, how he's talking about ummm the brok . . . vision of broken bladed glory, and you know, talking about how men were too sophisticated now to have battles and war and then you . . . the end where he's just fighting instinctively.

Sarah: OK.

Danny: Where they . . . when . . . the battle where they said that he was a war demon or something like that.

Tom: Uh huh.

Sarah: OK.

This passage, typical of the language of autonomous and semi-autonomous writing groups, dramatizes the linguistic transactions that occur in these groups. Danny modifies his original statement as a result of a complex negotiation with his peers. The term *man* is expanded to include self-confidence, respect for others, and finally heroism, so that Danny is able to make new connections between his subject and the language of the novel he is writing about. The language of the questions posed, the suggestions made, and the text of *The Red Badge of Courage* all intermingle with Danny's original statement so that the words Danny writes with his borrowed pencil are demonstrably half someone else's.

Danny and his peers rely, as do most writing group participants, on talking to one another to create their own vernacular, but the text Danny ultimately submits takes written form. This movement between talking and writing stands in contrast to another dichotomy contained in the received tradition of language study. I refer to the dichotomy of speaking and writing. Theorists in a number of fields define speaking and writing in terms of oppositions or similarities, but very few consider how they interact. Linguists have identified distinctive features of speaking and writing, noting that speech is oriented to hearing, is ephemeral and immediate, and occurs as a natural part of human development in all cultures. Writing, on the other hand, is oriented to sight, has permanence, can communicate across time and space, and requires special instruction (De Vito; Hanneman; Horowitz and Newman; Woolbert). While these features are unambiguous enough, analyses of more specific aspects often lead to conflicting statements about differences between speech and writing. Studies of sentence length, passive constructions, type-token ratios, and personal references have produced conflicting results, with one researcher claiming that speech has more of a particular feature and another researcher asserting that writing has the majority (Einhorn; Green; Mann; Portnoy).

Psychologists have likewise come to differing conclusions about the speaking-writing relationship. David Olson, for example, argues that writing (as opposed to speaking) aids cognitive development because the permanence and linearity of writing lead to increased ability to discern the literal meaning of sentences (to distinguish what was said from what was meant), and this ability, in turn, increases problem-solving skill. Scribner and Cole, because of their research among the Vai people where writing and schooling are separated, disagree, claiming that the cognitive abilities credited to writing are actually the result of formal education, and that writing does not, in itself, enhance cognition.

Some of the conflicting findings of linguists and psychologists result from the conditions under which they were produced. A number of investigations of distinctive features, for example, used a small number of subjects speaking and writing in one situation and then attempted to generalize to all people in all situations. The differences between working in a culture where formal education and writing are intertwined and in a culture where they can be separated helps explain the differing perspectives of Olson and Scribner

and Cole. Finally, however, these conflicts originate from a dichotomous view of speaking and writing.

Several recent studies have moved away from this dichotomous
position. Vachek, drawing on a careful examination of speaking and
writing, claims that they are "functionally complementary" systems.
Prince questions the explicit/less explicit and decontextualized/
contextualized distinctions between writing and speaking. Tannen,
recanting her earlier statements about separate oral and literate
strategies, argues that oral strategies underlie successful writing,
and Villanueva provides an empirical basis for this claim by demonstrating how writers use sound in their work. In the largest sense,
Tannen and Villanueva operate outside the speaking/writing dichotomy, and they acknowledge, with Vygotsky and Bakhtin, the dialogic relationship between internal and external language.

This dialogic relationship betweeeen speech and writing characterizes writing groups because participants combine the two, as
they did in the excerpt quoted above. The conversation began with
the words Danny had prepared, moved through a series of negotiations to create a vernacular that all members could accept, and then
the conversation continued in writing as Danny recorded the newly
created ideas. In addition to creating an interaction between speech
and writing, peer response posits meaning in dialogic terms. Danny
comes to a new understanding of his topic (a new meaning) as a result
of the group's discussion. Participants make false starts, hesitate,
circle back, and then hit upon an expanded definition of *man* that
satisfies all of them; they generate meaning. This demonstration of
the making of meaning illustrates Vygotsky's claim about the *sense* of
words. A dictionary definition of *man* or even of *becoming a man*
could not capture the meaning encapsulated in that phrase by the
end of the discussion. The initial questions and statements of doubt
("Do you?" "I don't think . . .") lead Danny to invest *man* with the
meaning of *prove himself* and Tom's statement about "making it
through" adds dimensions of surviving and enduring. Sarah enlarges
this with the concept of generativity as she adds the idea of having
something to tell his children. Sarah then contributes the idea of
commanding respect ("be looked up to"), and the group settles on
the term *hero*. Danny draws on the language of the text for concepts
of cynicism ("broken bladed glory"), automation ("fighting instinctively"), and fearlessness ("war demon") so that the sense of the

word *hero* includes at least proving oneself, enduring, generativity, commanding respect, cynicism, automation, and fearlessness. This group of individuals working with a common text thus creates a *sense* for *man* or *hero* that reflects the context in which they exist.

In creating meaning, writing groups employ a wide range of language functions. M. A. K. Halliday's delineation of three functions of adult language describes the range. These include the ideational, the interpersonal, and the textual. The ideational expresses the writer's experience, thought, and knowledge and not only "specifies the available options in meaning but also determines the nature of their structural realization" (39). It is the "content" of writing. The interpersonal expresses the writer's relationship to audience and subject, a relationship into which both judgments and attitudes enter. Personal expression and social interaction find voice in the interpersonal function, and its uses are unlimited. Through this function language can be made to "approve, and disapprove; to express belief, opinion, doubt; to include in the social group, or exclude from it; to ask and answer; to express personal feelings; to achieve intimacy" (41). The textual function produces coherent, cohesive, and living texts that can be distinguished from dictionary entries. It gives language texture by providing "the remaining strands of meaning potential to be woven into the fabric of linguistic structure" (42).

Transcripts demonstrate that all three of these functions appear in writing groups. In the excerpt quoted above, for example, the ideational function centers on the question of whether "becoming a man" is the central issue for Henry in *The Red Badge of Courage*. As students make suggestions and ask questions, they help Danny shape and develop ideas. The exchanges among participants make the interpersonal dimension of writing central. By asking difficult and penetrating questions, Danny's peers remind him of the writer's continuing need to attend to the reader/audience. When Sarah asks, "So what are you going to use to back it up?" she helps Danny consider the textual function in his work because her question reminds Danny that he must produce a coherent and cohesive text. These conversations help writers generate language about language. If we assume, with Kenneth Bruffee, that writing is "internalized social and public talk made public again," then the talk of writing groups, because it includes such a broad range of functions, creates a vernacular to be internalized for the members' future use.

This vernacular language often facilitates formative evaluation among writers. Formative evaluation refers to evaluation that occurs during the process of writing and can be contrasted with summative evaluation that occurs when writing has been completed. Formative evaluation contributes to the eventual quality of writing while summative evaluation assigns a value to that quality. Writing groups are frequently credited with helping participants to produce better writing than their nonparticipating counterparts, and the vernacular of formative evaluation contributes directly to this better writing. As I have explained elsewhere, typical evaluation often neglects the meaning dimension, concentrating instead on the most superficial aspects of writing. Consequently, great numbers of instructor hours invested in "correcting" often have little effect (Gere, "Written Composition"). Writing groups, in contrast, focus on creating meaning through dialogue among participants, and this creation enables writers to re vision their work, improving it substantially.

This creation of meaning assumes, of course, that a writing group is autonomous or at least semi-autonomous. As the conversation among Danny, Sarah, and Tom illustrates, the power of the group derives from its freedom to create its own language. Critics of writing groups sometimes overlook this. Tom Newkirk, for example, found that peer evaluation differs significantly from that of instructors. Newkirk explains the motivation for his study: "If students approach peers' writing with values, interests, and emphases different from those of writing instructors, the status of the peer response becomes problematical" ("Direction and Misdirection" 301). In saying this, Newkirk conflates formative and summative evaluation, implying that writing groups should determine the value of a piece of writing rather than contribute to its development. In addition, Newkirk fails to deal with the issue of authority, the feature that determines whether classroom writing groups remain nonautonomous or become semi-autonomous. As long as authority for "values, interests, and emphases" remains the sole province of the instructor, writing groups will remain nonautonomous and unable to develop the vernacular that enables them to become their own best critics.

Obstacles to semi-autonomous writing groups also arise from the traditional patterns of language use in classrooms. Studies of linguistic transactions in classrooms reveal that teachers do most of the talking and have access to a much wider range of language functions than do students. Bellack and his associates found that teachers dominate the "structuring, soliciting and reacting" (46), while students do a majority of the responding. In addition, teachers speak longer and more frequently than do students (238). This limited access to language functions has direct consequences for students. Barnes found that the questions teachers ask secondary school students constrain students' thought and participation in class ("Language"). Flanders observed that teachers' language influences both pupil achievement and involvement. Mishler examined the language of elementary school classrooms and found no substantive or logical continuity between student comments because "the connections between responses are mediated by the teacher" (274). Sinclair and Coulthard's investigations revealed a high degree of rigidity in teacher-pupil interactions. Teachers typically move through a series of carefully planned steps and limit students to responses framed by cues such as "Wouldn't you agree that . . . " to which students respond in the affirmative whether or not they understand or agree.

Teaching does, of course, imply guiding and shaping students' activities, but it does not require limiting students' access to language. This limitation suggests problems when one considers research on the relationship between language and learning. Although they disagree on its ultimate source and nature, both Vygotsky and Piaget see language as contributing directly to learning. Through verbalizing, persons explore their world and make sense of it. Furthermore, empirical studies indicate that language plays a major part in problem solving. Gagne and Smith, for example, found that requiring individuals to verbalize while practicing a three-circle problem led to superior performance. Subsequent studies (see Goor and Sommerfield; Carmean and Weir) support claims for verbalizing's contributions to problem solving. These studies, combined with the theories of Vygotsky and Piaget, suggest that limiting students to a small range of linguistic responses compromises their opportunities for classroom learning. Writing groups, in contrast to many other class activities, give students access to a wide range of linguistic responses, and as Danny, Sarah, and Tom demonstrated, writing groups enable students to engage in negotiations that help them solve the problems of their writing.

As a result of this negotiation within writing groups, participants develop metalanguage about writing. Metalanguage, or language about language, contributes significantly to what cognitive psychologists call metacognition (Sternberg, "What Should Intelligence Tests Test"). Current discussions of human intelligence argue that metacognition (the ability to monitor one's own thinking) constitutes a major factor in mental ability because people who are aware of how they think perform better than those who are not (Sternberg, *Beyond IQ* 13–14). In tests of reading, for example, time allocation and strategy selection (strategies such as prioritizing difficult or important passages) differentiate levels of performance. Individuals who allocate time judiciously and sort tasks according to difficulty perform better than those who do not (Sternberg, *Beyond IQ* 241–57). Vygotsky's work on intrapsychological processes likewise underlines the importance of this language about language. For Vygotsky intralinguistic relationships describe ways that language operates on itself, and he claimed that these relationships play an important role in concept development (Wertsch 156). Vygotsky's theory thus supports the idea that talking about language in writing groups helps participants understand writing more fully.

When writing group members discuss how transitions will be effected, how an idea will be developed, how introductions and conclusions will be handled, or how they will convey an idea, they use language to talk about language. A study of the language of classroom writing groups (Gere and Abbott) revealed that a high percentage of participants' comments focus on ways of writing. Group members offer one another directions on how to proceed with writing, saying things such as, "The introductory paragraph needs to describe the garden more completely," or, "The ending needs another sentence to feel finished." They ask questions: "How are you going to lead into her saying that?" or "How are you defining determinism?" They make statements about the nature of writing: "I can't write the introduction until I've decided what the main section will say," or "Hemingway used short sentences like that." Group members also use a significant amount of terminology to describe forms of writing acceptable in a given community. They discuss concepts such as "introduction," "conclusion," and "transition," and they explore ideas of style and organization. In addition, they refer to their habits of drafting and revising.

This metalanguage or language about language aids the growth of critical skills so frequently attributed to writing groups. Lagana, for example, found that students who participate in writing groups develop better critical thinking skills than do students who do not participate in such groups. As Kenneth Bruffee puts it, writing groups have a large and positive effect on "the faculty of judgment" ("Brooklyn Plan" 453). In talking about their processes and forms of composing, group members become better judges of their own and others' writing.

Finally, then, the linguistic transactions of writing groups foster development because they are primarily language about language. But the value of these transactions—and even the process by which they occur—becomes apparent only from the perspective of a non-Cartesian epistemology such that in which Vygotsky frames his theories. When language is perceived as a conduit between mind and matter, as it must be in Cartesian epistemology, then writing groups remain peripheral. But when language is perceived as a social construct central to knowing—as Vygotsky claims—then writing groups become essential: essential because learning to write means learning to use the language of a given community, and writing groups provide a forum in which individuals can practice and internalize this language.

Part 3

Implications

5

Practical Directions

KNOWING SOMETHING OF THE HISTORY AND THEORY OF WRITING
groups leads to two sets of implications, one practical and one theoretical. This chapter deals with practical questions while the next
considers theoretical issues.

To discuss practical issues is not, however, to offer a formula for
establishing and maintaining effective writing groups. As the history
of writing groups in this country illustrates, there is no one "right"
way to proceed. Questions of size, procedures, timing, genre, membership, and context have been answered variously by individual
groups. Workshops such as those instituted at the University of Iowa
and the Breadloaf Writers' Conference share with literary societies
and women's clubs a large number of respondents. One advantage of
this size, usually twenty-five to thirty people, is that no one individual is reponsible for making a great number of negative comments,
and the cumulative effect of repetition can be convincing to the author. Conversely, smaller groups, such as those found in many classrooms and some self-improvement groups, have the advantage of intimacy and a virtual guarantee that all participants will be motivated
toward and active in group work.

Some groups elect critics to respond to writers' work while others
rely upon spontaneous responses of the whole group. In some groups
authors read aloud from written drafts; in others the participants read
drafts silently to themselves and then offer either oral or written responses. Sometimes authors are responsible for making notes on
comments offered, and in other cases those responding provide written copies of their comments. In school-sponsored writing groups
the role of the teacher likewise varies. Some teachers participate

equally with students, sharing their own writing and offering their comments along with students; some moderate critique sessions, underlining comments with which they agree and screening out those they think less appropriate; some leave groups entirely on their own, relying on reports from group moderators about group progress; and still others move from group to group, monitoring behavior, offering suggestions, and modeling effective responses when groups falter.

Use of time likewise varies from one group to another. One group may operate on a strict schedule, allocating a certain number of minutes to each individual in the group and appointing a time-keeper to ensure that all participants receive a hearing. Another may proceed more informally, allowing as much time as an individual author wishes for reading and responding to the work. School-sponsored writing groups usually operate within the constraints of scheduled class time, but sometimes instructors adjust by having classes meet for double sessions or allocating successive days to writing groups to make up for the limitations imposed by a a bell ringing after forty-five or fifty minutes. Some groups meet weekly, others monthly, and still others seasonally (such as during the summer months).

Some writing groups concentrate on a single genre, such as poetry or drama, while others include writers who work in a variety of genres. Those who limit group work to a single genre usually maintain that a mixture is distracting, while those who encourage several genres claim that the variety offers participants multiple perspectives. Predictably, group procedures sometimes change with genre. Participants who usually read their work aloud may, for example, distribute copies of poems so everyone can attend to visual effects, line breaks, and other non-aural aspects of poetry. Likewise, groups that usually read one another's work silently may switch to oral reading for dramatic scripts where the sound of the language is more important.

Although groups take a variety of forms they can be categorized into three main types—autonomous, semi-autonomous and non-autonomous—depending upon the locus and degree of authority. The voluntary constitution of writing groups within literary societies, young men's associations, women's clubs, and in myriad other self-sponsored gatherings identifies them as autonomous. Authority resides within individual members of autonomous groups because they choose to join other writers with whom they are friendly, share common interests, backgrounds, or needs. Autonomous writing groups depend upon members who are willing to give away, temporarily at least, authority over their own writing, indicating that they respect and trust one another enough to surrender their language to one another's critical scrutiny. The sense of empowerment—whether among culturally deprived students, economically disadvantaged workers, socially constrained women, or any individuals who seek more control over their own writing—characteristic of writing groups both past and present results from this simultaneous giving and receiving of authority.

Classroom writing groups are either semi-autonomous or non-autonomous depending upon the instructor's willingness and ability to provide students opportunities to emulate autonomous groups. In nonautonomous groups students never experience the empowerment of using language collaboratively to generate new understandings because the instructor fails to give them the authority to do so. Preparation (or more commonly lack of it), group functioning, assignments or tasks, and evaluation all contrive to prevent members of nonautonomous groups from assuming authority. Instructors have many ways of enabling student to take on a portion of the authority enjoyed by autonomous groups, and when they are successful, classroom groups can become semi-autonomous. This means that individual members experience much of the empowerment characteristic of autonomous groups, but they can never, because of the authority invested in the educational institution and its representative the instructor, become truly autonomous. The following discussion examines autonomous and semi-autonomous writing groups, highlighting the areas where they differ in locus and degree of authority.

For autonomous groups the first issue is finding individual members. Individuals become members of self-sponsored writing groups in a variety of ways, but now, as in the past, most form around similarities of education, class, and goals. College literary societies grew from the efforts of relatively privileged young men seeking a kind of intellectual endeavor not available in the college curriculum, while apprentices who formed self-improvement societies had more practical aims of raising their status in society. Similarly, class markers such as her husband's occupation frequently determined which club a woman might join, but other clubs placed more emphasis on shared goals such as study of specific issues or publication of members' writing. Today's self-sponsored writing groups follow similar patterns of formation, and goals continue to play a large role. Writers whose primary concern is publication, for example, often discourage members who write for their own pleasure because these members may not be "serious" enough. No matter how they happen to join a particular group, individuals in self-sponsored writing groups possess an authority and autonomy unequalled by any school-sponsored group.

One manifestation of this difference appears in the way school-sponsored writing groups are formed. Dividing students into groups is not the first step in establishing classroom writing groups, but when it does occur teachers play a major role in deciding who works with whom. Group composition results from juggling constraints of size (usually four to seven members), heterogeneity (of gender, writing ability, and personality type), and configuration (assigned roles such as recorder or chair). Instructors interested in creating semi-autonomous groups give considerable thought to balancing these factors in a way that passes a measure of authority on to students.

Some teachers minimize their influence by allowing students to determine the membership of their own groups. Others organize students into groups with an eye to diversity in writing ability, gender, and interpersonal skills, and still others have elaborate systems for combining student and teacher preferences. They may, for example, ask students to indicate one or two classmates with whom they would especially like to work and then construct sociograms, placing everyone in a group with at least one preferred individual. Such systems allow students some self-determination without compromising the teacher's concern for diversity in each group.

As all students and all teachers know, authority finally rests with the instructor, but students who have some choice about group membership can move toward a semi-autonomy. A more important contribution to the development of authority among participants in classroom writing groups lies in the preparation for these groups.

Writing groups, both in and out of school, proceed in many right ways, and no single set of guidelines will be effective in all times and circumstances. There are, however, some clear ways for writing groups to go wrong. Most of these fall under the general category of beginning too soon or without sufficient commitment. School-sponsored writing groups require months of preparation, and when I meet teachers who say, "Oh, I tried writing groups and they didn't work," I begin by asking about the preparation.

Establishing trust, developing collaborative skills or discovering those developed outside the classroom, and learning to critique writing constitute the preparation necessary for classroom writing groups. All writers find sharing their work risky because their language is vulnerable to attack by others. Because one's language is such an intricate part of oneself, an attack on language constitutes an attack on the self, and all writers, even those in elementary school, are wary of exposing their language to the criticism of others. Being asked to change one's language means being asked to change oneself, to leave one community and join another, and the fact that this change is the goal of writing groups does not make the process of changing any easier or less threatening. Accordingly, teachers can prepare for writing groups by transforming the class into a community where all members feel secure. This means establishing a climate where put-downs are disallowed, where people are encouraged to express their ideas without fear of recrimination, and where diversity is appreciated, not deprecated.

Teachers can create a supportive classroom community in many ways. They can set an example of respect for others by modeling it in their dealings with all students, and they can use a variety of activities to encourage positive sharing. I have found that asking students to introduce one another or to respond briefly to questions or quotations as part of daily attendance routines quickly establishes the importance and possibility of hearing from everyone in the class (Gere, Roots 222–28). Establishing tasks that depend upon group cooperation, requiring frequent reading of student writing to the whole class (either short anonymous observations written when students enter the class and read aloud by the teacher or selections chosen by students from their journals) and including opportunities for role-playing, help solidify a positive classroom climate. Although it is crucial to introduce many community-building activities early in the life of a given class, the need for community building extends beyond the first weeks of the term. Classroom communities, like all other living bodies, need continuing nourishment.

With college and graduate school students, successful writing groups do sometimes function in the absence of supportive classroom communities, but students at this level may have enough confidence in their own abilities to be able to work without a great deal of emotional support. Still, absence of feelings of community and trust in a group exacts a price, one Don Murray describes this way:

> Writing programs usually see workshop as the test by fire, the sort of varsity scrimmage or wargame in which a guy is tested. I am being purposely sexist. Only a few years ago I heard a writer say, "She didn't have the balls to publish in workshop!" That was a point that made me think about my workshop teaching. I heard that quote the same week that a piece of mine was attacked in a workshop of my peers. I knew the lead didn't work; I'd tried all sorts of ways to find a lead that worked, but when a colleague attacked the lead I defended it. (letter)

For Murray the unsupportive emotional climate led to vocal defensiveness, while for other authors it may lead to withdrawal; in any case, the result is the same. Writing groups established without attention to or concern for a prior sense of trust among members risk diminished performances from all participants.

Although necessary, establishing a sense of community does not constitute sufficient preparation for a classroom writing group. Students also need to learn how to work together in groups. Tom Hilgers, who has done extensive research on classroom writing groups, asserts: "The mere creation of collaborative settings for writers is not alone going to generate effective writing. Collaborative skills, like writing skills, must be learned" (12). Learning collaborative skills means, among other things, mastering the social skills needed to work with others in a group and developing the ability to identify and solve problems. Social skills such as stating one's opinion and listening carefully to the contributions of others can be taught prior to establishing writing groups, as instructors encourage class discussion.

If students learn the importance of listening carefully to others before they work in writing groups, they will be more able to function well in such groups. As a preliminary students can develop their listening skills with class dictation exercises. If the instructor reads passages aloud for students to copy, students increase both accuracy and retention of listening (Gere, *Roots* 224). A more difficult and important way of enhancing students' listening skills is for instructors to move away from the traditional recitation style of class discussion where all comments are directed to the instructor (and students make little effort to respond to one another). As Mishler has observed, this type of recitation leads to classroom language where all logical connections remain the teacher's responsibility. If instructors insist that students direct comments to the whole class, respond to one another, and refrain from relying on the teacher to make connections between statements and answer all questions, students' listening skills will improve dramatically. Students will learn to extract meaning from one another's language rather than merely waiting for their opportunity to impress the instructor. In the process they will recognize that their peers give classroom comments careful attention and will become more willing to take risks with their own language.

As students develop listening skills, they become more able to engage in productive problem solving. The ability to identify and solve problems in writing groups takes the specific form of being able to locate and offer constructive suggestions for problems in writing. This means that group members need practice in responding to writing—the kind of practice that teachers can provide by moderating whole-class critique sessions. In such sessions the instructor can highlight useful comments made by students and model others. Implicit in such highlighting will be an acknowledgment of the close relationship between language and feeling, a relationship that contributes to the power inherent in writing groups. In some cases, of course, writing groups remain whole-class activities, but instructor modeling at the outset can make such groups more effective. Another form of modeling involves inviting practiced writing group members to do a "fish bowl" demonstration of their procedures for a class, allowing time for questions from students after the demonstration. Developing listening skills and problem-solving abilities prepares students to participate effectively in writing groups, but the crucial ingredient is commitment.

Teaching commitment to writing groups among students who are required to participate is probably impossible, but commitment can be caught if not taught. Among instructors who tell me their writing groups failed I find a high percentage of diffidence or uncertainty.

That is, I find instructors who put students into writing groups because they think it's "good" to do so, not because they know their value first-hand and believe in it. Instructors who introduce writing groups successfully usually are those who have participated in writing groups themselves and know the benefits for their own writing. Part of their success may derive from the fact that such instructors can, by drawing on their own experience, anticipate problems and offer more useful guidance than their inexperienced colleagues. Nevertheless, their commitment to writing groups takes precedence with students, who, like all subjugated groups, read their superiors' feelings expertly.

"Commitment" can be rendered less abstract when put into action. Instructors who claim belief in writing groups give life to that statement by the kind of authority they pass on to students. One of the least effective groups I have observed, for example, worked in a classroom where the teacher asked students to respond to finished pieces of writing. Although they never articulated their complaint, students knew that they didn't have a "real" task; the comments they made would not shape a revision because the writing was completed. Despite her protestations to the contrary, this instructor demonstrated how to make writing groups go wrong. Because this instructor failed to invest their work with the authority of shaping future drafts, students failed to "catch" commitment to the work of the groups.

Another more subtle form of teacher commitment to writing groups centers on the teacher's willingness to take on a new role, not to abdicate responsibility but to assume it differently. One of the critical salvos most frequently aimed at writing groups addresses the issue of teacher responsibility. Critics usually assert that writing groups exist to make teacher's lives easier, pointing to article titles such as "The Efficiency of Student Correction of Compositions" (Tressler), "A Practical Proposition to Take the Drudgery out of the Teaching of Freshman Composition and to Restore to the Teacher His Pristine Measure in Teaching" (Bernadette), "When the Teacher Stops Teaching" (Putz), or "What Students Can Do To Take the Burden off You" (Hardaway) to sustain their claims. Higley's parody of the writing group meeting in which students carry out a desultory conversation about procedures, making comments such as, "What we're supposed to do is say what we think about the writing without taking time to make it up," and, "It flowed just right" (682) likewise provides evidence for critics. One group member sits with his head on the desk during the entire session, and after one paper has been discussed, the group decides to take a break. This parody typifies the teacher irresponsibility suggested by some article titles (although it is rarely the substance of these articles) and criticized by those who doubt the value of writing groups. The students portrayed in this parody demonstrate no understanding of or commitment to their task, a sure sign their their instructor has not prepared them sufficiently for writing groups.

Successful classroom writing groups depend upon teachers committed to preparing students with the necessary social and intellectual skills. When this preparation is effective, students become proprietary about their writing groups. In observing school-sponsored groups, I heard a number of students insist that they could not complete their assignments unless the instructor gave them time to work with their groups. Members of self-sponsored groups typically have considerably less overt preparation, but the lack of school-imposed requirements and timetables does not exempt self-sponsored writing groups from all problems. It is more complicated to form a self-sponsored group. Potential participants do not always appear, and writers often roam local conferences looking for others interested in sharing their work. Even when they find one another, members of self-sponsored writing groups wrestle with the issue of commitment. Without the external pressure of school requirements, some individuals find it difficult to attend regular meetings and to prepare writing on agreed-upon schedules. Still, self-sponsored groups need less preparation because a good portion of preparation for classroom writing groups deals, directly or indirectly, with transferring authority from teacher to students, a transfer unnecessary in groups where individual members start from positions of authority.

Yet, as history demonstrates, self-sponsored groups rarely rely entirely upon their own resources. College literary societies leaned upon faculty members; young men's associations evolved into Lyceum groups, partly because the latter provided more structure than individual groups could manage; local chapters of the Chautauqua Literary and Scientific Circle relied upon a prescribed outline to guide their study; and individual women's clubs joined a national federation that provided more resources and structure than could be generated by a single group. In various ways and with differing degrees of success, self-sponsored writing groups of previous generations sought preparation or at least structure from individuals or groups beyond themselves. Individual members' commitment to writing groups grew from the mixtures of need, friendship, and common interests or background that led them to join these groups. In the absence of instructors who can train them in group processes and critical responses, participants devise their own ways of proceeding or they draw upon published resources such as Peter Elbow's *Writing without Teachers*. This usually means that some form of individual or corporate leadership emerges, assuring that all members understand and adhere to agreed-upon procedures.

Commitment is more crucial and easier to assess in self-sponsored groups because, in the absence of school requirements, participants vote with their feet. When participants miss meetings frequently or come unprepared, they are usually signaling a lack of commitment to the group. Some groups, in an effort to insure continuity, will stipulate responsibilities in advance. This was the case with women's clubs, which frequently published programs for the forthcoming year. Other groups try to relieve the burden of continuing responsibility by agreeing to meet for a specified period—such as five months—and then renegotiating for another specified period of time.

Regular attendance does not, of course, provide sufficent support for group survival. Just as is true of classroom groups, commitment takes subtle as well as obvious forms. Bringing "dead" writing, writing on which the author is no longer actively working, can kill a group as quickly as failure to attend. Just as students "know" when an instructor genuinely cares about the success of writing groups, so participants can sense when an author is no longer engaged by a given selection.

Even when preparation and commitment are adequate, no writing group can function effectively without a clear and appropriate task. For groups of mature and experienced writers, directives such as "critique one another's writing" may be adequate, but for most other groups more specific directions are necessary. In school-sponsored writing groups instructors can, employ one of several methods for specifying what groups should concentrate on. Instructors can, as Linda Clifton suggests, provide models of the type of writing students are currently working on and ask students to draw on these to develop terminology for defining success in a particular assignment. Students then use these criteria in their writing groups. Alternatively, an instructor can simply review previous relevant lessons before groups assemble so students have a clear idea of what they should look for in one another's writing. Some instructors find it useful to provide students with a list of questions to be asked about a draft: "What is the main point?" "Who is likely to read this?" "Is each point supported adequately?" "Where can the language be made more clear?" Still others follow Harvey Wiener's advice and ask all students to list the two or three questions they need answered about their drafts so they can continue writing. The instructor then collects the questions for everyone to see (56).

To be genuinely effective a writing group's task must also be appropriate to the group's level of functioning. That is, tasks need to be calibrated to what Vygotsky calls the zone of proximal development. In the most general terms, this means giving students assignments they cannot accomplish independently but can, with help from their friends, complete successfully. The specific zone of proximal development for a given group can be identified only by a teacher who works closely with students much as a coach does, watching, encouraging, and suggesting. Such instructors will know how well students can handle features such as "detail" or "transitions," and they will not tasks that push students to move just beyond what they can handle comfortably on their own.

These specifications set an agenda for classroom writing groups, but instructors usually need to go beyond this and detail how the group should proceed. To be effective these details must be very specific, and they should be modeled for students. For example, if students are to read drafts aloud and receive oral comments, they should be told how time is to be divided among group members, the number of times a selection should be read, the form of note taking that will aid effective response, how authors should introduce their writing, and whether authors should receive written comments in addition to oral ones. If each group has a chair or leader, that person's duties should be clarified. Among the functions instructors can assign to chairs are timekeeper, attendance taker, convener, arbitrator, and recorder. If the instructor requires written reports from each chair, the form and content of these reports should be explained.

Others will ask students to fill out rating sheets on which criteria are listed. Sometimes these criteria are specific to a given piece of writing, such as "effective details" and "need more information" for descriptive writing, and sometimes they are generic criteria such as "what I learned from this writing" or "these examples and details clarified or developed the central idea of the essay." Others argue that these sheets become a form of busy work through which students plod mechanically, paying little attention to the writing itself.

In self-sponsored groups the task is both more vague and more specific. The goals—whether self-improvement, freedom from domestic isolation, publication, or a combination of these—that lead a group to form in the first place usually define the task. Groups interested in self- improvement often adopt a course of study that focuses on a specific area (such as "Medieval Art" or "Public Policy in a Nuclear Age") and assign members to write on specific topics. The terms in which such writing is discussed usually concentrate more on content than form, although records of some women's clubs include discussion of writing style. Groups that take publication as their primary goal often give members "assignments" by reporting on the current interests of certain publishers.

Original goals of self-sponsored groups frequently provide a general outline of the task, but, unlike classrooms where instructors provide models and specific guidelines for procedures, accomplishing the given task is often difficult. One set of difficulties comes from defensiveness among participants. Author defensiveness poses a potentially greater problem in self-sponsored groups than it does in school-sponsored ones. With the mediating force of teachers missing, some individuals attach unjustified value to their own writing, defending it furiously against all criticism. The other form of this defensiveness appears in preceding all readings of one's writing with extremely self-deprecating remarks. Certainly this problem is not unique to self-sponsored groups, because students frequently assume the same postures, but without a teacher to intervene, defensive authors can cripple groups. Sometimes groups adopt a light-hearted approach such as the "one apology rule," specifying that authors are allowed to apologize for their work only once during the life of the group, while others impose and enforce prohibitions against author comments.

Disgruntled comments scattered throughout records of literary societies, women's clubs, and other non-school organizations indicate how difficult it is for self-sponsored writing groups to agree upon and adhere to a set of procedures. Mighican's Literary Adelphi sometimes held private critique sessions, presumably to avoid the contentiousness inherent in more public discussions of a work's quality. Minutes of the Seattle Writers' Club contain frequent entries about disagreements among members, difficulties in dealing with a few dominating individuals, and concern that the critic's role had been abrogated by the group. Often the actual recording of a complaint provided sufficient relief, and in other cases groups took action—such as private critique sessions—to alleviate the problem.

When participants are adequately prepared and tasks clear and appropriate, writing groups function best with little interference from outsiders. In school-sponsored groups, teachers may need to attend to logistics such as providing adequate space and designing an effective arrangement of furniture for a number of groups to meet simultaneously, but once groups begin meeting, instructors need do little except monitor groups to see if they are progressing on schedule. Some instructors choose to join one group while others move from group to group, but as Wiener cautions, instructors can undermine the group's authority, and when groups are actually meeting, the best teacher is "the seemingly most idle teacher" (58). The continuing success of self-sponsored writing groups offers further proof that instructors needn't hover over classroom groups.

When writing groups have finished a session, or perhaps a series of sessions, another aspect of their work remains. I refer to evaluation or, as Barnes and Todd call it, *debriefing*. A quick survey of publications on writing groups (see part 1 of the Bibliography) reveals that most concentrate on claiming the value of or procedures for establishing these groups, but very few discuss evaluation after a group meeting. Yet it is evaluation that transforms the work of writing groups into the kind of learning that enables participants to negotiate their way, as Kenneth Bruffee describes it, into the normal discourse of "knowledgeable peers." By discussing the issues that have arisen in their writing groups, explaining what they have learned, and exploring unresolved issues, participants learn to monitor their own thinking and evaluate their own progress. If instructors lead such discussions skillfully, students can also learn to see relationships among issues as they, for example, recognize similarities among reports from several groups. They can learn to use evidence more convincingly as they offer substantiation for their observations, and they can begin to construct hypotheses as they consider the similarities and differences of what is said. They can, in other words, engage in a variety of cognitive activites that foster learning.

Self-sponsored writing groups may lack structured opportunities for evaluation, but many develop informal substitutes for teacher-directed discussions. My own writing group, for example, has evolved a time for "smoking in the hall" after the evening's readings and responses are finished. During this time participants raise questions, draw conclusions, and talk about what the group is doing at a level of abstraction impossible during the group's "official" working session. Written records of self-sponsored writing groups include little such informal conversation, but the origins of both school- and self-sponsored writing groups suggest the continuing importance attached to evaluative thinking. Literary societies, after all, focused on debate before they turned to writing, and this practice of looking at two sides of an issue created a legacy of critical thinking. Franklin's Junto and the various men's and women's groups that built upon its tradition likewise valued the kind of close examination that fosters intellectual development.

Writing groups, then, do not fit comfortably within any given mold or model—they succeed, or fail, in many ways. But in the most general terms we can assert that they are more likely to succeed when groups are sufficiently prepared and committed, when appropriate tasks are clear and/or agreed upon by all participants, and when debriefing or evaluation is built into the life of the group.

6

Theories of Literacy

WHILE PRACTICAL IMPLICATIONS OF AND FOR WRITING GROUPS extend in multiple directions, the theoretical implications take more monolithic form. The single line out of which theoretical implications extend has its roots in the founding purposes of these groups. Whether they began as part of extracurricular groups such as the Female Mutual Improvement Society and the Junto or as part of academic groups such as Zelo and Tabbard; whether initiated in 1771 or in yesterday's classroom; whether populated by adults or school children; whether sponsored by group members or required by teachers—writing groups exist to improve the writing of their members. As such these groups contribute to the development of literacy, and literacy stands at their center. The theoretical implications of writing groups, then, extend into an understanding of literacy—its meaning, purposes, and development.

Discussions of literacy have expanded rapidly in the decades since Jack Goody's 1968 assertion that "surprisingly little attention has been given to the way in which it [literacy] has influenced the social life of mankind" ("Literacy" 1). Goody could substantiate his claim by noting that although humans have been literate for more than 5,000 years, published studies of literacy at the end of the nineteenth century numbered only thirty. Some of this expansion has, no doubt, come in response to the media-inflamed "literacy crisis" of the early 1970s, but the more substantial portion has emerged as scholars in anthropology, political science, economics, history, and English studies have reached beyond the traditional boundaries of their respective fields to examine the nature of literacy. Accordingly, the meaning of "literacy" has changed in recent years.

Historically, *literacy* meant ability to read and write, and researchers frequently took signatures on marriage certificates or other legal documents as evidence of literacy (Cippola). More recently, in the United States, for example, literacy has been defined as completion of a specified number of years of formal education or ability to complete set tasks requiring reading and writing. Implicit in all such skill-based definitions of literacy is a technological meaning. To define literacy in terms of skills is to see it as a technology.

Indeed, a number of theorists have made this claim explicitly. Jack Goody, for example, describes literacy as a technology of intellect that, among other things, enables one to "compare side by side utterances that have been made at different times and places" (*Domestication* 11–12). John Oxenham, following Goody's lead, defines literacy as "simply a technology invented for certain practical purposes" (84), and Walter Ong claims that "writing (and especially alphabetic writing) is a technology, calling for the use of tools and other equipment" (81).

Those who assign a technology/skills meaning to literacy assume that the technology of literacy has clear and direct effects on mental functioning. They claim that people who have the ability to read and write can accomplish complex cognitive tasks that are impossible for illiterates. Classical scholar Eric Havelock goes so far as to claim literacy's benefits for the human race. For Havelock, the development of an alphabetic writing system was a pivotal event leading to the spread of literacy in post-Homeric Greece and changing the basic forms of human memory. Walter Ong echoes this view when he claims that "technologies are not mere exterior aids but also interior transformations of consciousness. . . . writing heightens consciousness" (82) and asserts that the printing press gave rise to a new form of intellectual inquiry. Specifically, according to advocates of the literacy as technology theory, literacy enables abstract thought. Greenfield and Bruner assert this relationship, claiming that "writing is practice in the use of linguistic contexts as independent of immediate reference [thereby enabling linguistic manipulation]. . . . Once thought is freed from the concrete situation the way is clear for symbolic manipulation and for Piaget's stage of formal operation in which the real becomes a sub-set of the possible" (175). Goody and Watt, drawing on their work in Africa, claim that "writing establishes a different kind of relationship between the word and its referent, a relationship that is more general and more abstract" and then describe the cognitive transformation that accompanies it (*Literacy* 44). David Olson likewise claims that learning to write changes individuals' cognitive processes.

This chorus of claims for the cognitive benefits of literacy leads, not surprisingly, to exhortations on the importance of spreading literacy. Oxenham, for instance, states that "the skills of literacy are so important to human mental development, the need for 'frontier pushers' so permanent, the possibility of discovering such people in 'deprived' or 'primitive communities' so far from negligible, that the opportunities for literacy should be rationed only for the gravest of reasons" (44). Underlying such exhortation is the assumption that the skill/technology of literacy enhances social and economic advancement, that it will liberate "those who remain fettered in their inescapable poverty and the darkness of ignorance" and help them join the literates "who master nature, share out the world's riches among themselves, and set out for the stars" (Maheu 112). Arguments made by directors of literacy programs throughout the world echo the idea if not the hyperbolic language of this claim.

As chapters 1 and 2 have explained, similar assumptions about literacy's capacity to improve minds or at least to enhance one's material circumstances led some individuals to form and/or participate in writing groups. Men whose socioeconomic status excluded them from extensive formal education joined with their peers in an effort to improve their literacy skills. Instructors who shared the conviction that writing groups led participants to produce better prose required their students to respond to one another's writing. Although history provides scanty information on the degree to which these efforts led to material change, the continuing appearance of classroom and self-sponsored groups in which literacy tasks played a central role testifies to the persistence of the technical/skills definition of literacy. The implications of this connection between a skills/technological definition of literacy and the work of writing groups do not extend very far. Rather, they move in a closed circle: individuals seek writing groups because they wish to improve them-

selves or their status in life, and the technological/skills meaning attached to literacy confirms the sensibility of their approach and the
value of their wish.

The theoretical thinness inherent in this view of literacy results in
part from the fact that the technological/skills definition of literacy
assigns no cultural content to literacy. It enables a dichotomous view
of the world wherein literate people can be clearly distinguished
from illiterates. The literates are capable of sophisticated thinking
and the illiterates remain forever at a lower level of mental functioning. Like a compass or a yardstick, this "objective" measure of hu-
manity can operate in every time and place to delineate two types of
people. Not surprisingly, advocates of the technical model of literacy, of whom Patricia Greenfield is an explicit example, draw on
Piaget's category of formal operations to describe the benefits of
standing on the literate side of "the great divide" between literates
and illiterates. The dichotomous view of literates and illiterates and
the unvarying qualities assigned to literacy belie the Cartesian epistemology within which this technical/skills definition operates.

The limitations of the Cartesian-based technology/skills definition
of literacy becomes apparent in its inability to address the formation of non-skills-oriented groups or the functioning of *any* autonomous or semi-autonomous writing group. Although they may have
been tangentially interested in improving their skills, many of the
students who joined literary societies were motivated by a complex
set of social, intellectual, and aesthetic concerns that extended beyond mere technique. In the largest sense, they wanted to create a
place for themselves in the academic community. Many women's
clubs were similarly constituted. Women with no visible need to improve their skills sought to join the larger intellectual comunity in
which ideas could be explored and discussed.

Similarly, the functioning of autonomous or semi-autonomous
writing groups cannot be explained in technical/skills terms because
the technical view of literacy presumes a pre-existing body of knowledge to be assimilated with language serving as the conduit. As
chapter 3 demonstrates, the collaborative learning of autonomous
and semi-autonomous groups can be explained only in terms of a
social constructivist view of knowledge that puts language at the
center because writing group participants work together to generate
much of what they learn. Likewise, as is shown in chapter 4, the

language development of writing groups proceeds along social, not individual, lines. Individuals internalize and transform the language they and their peers have generated, language that operates in what Vygotsky calls their zone of proximal development. Literacy defined as skills of encoding and decoding cannot account for collaborative learning or socially originated language development because autonomous skills can be transported across time and place with no reference to the particular commmunities in which they function, and collaborative learning and language development operate in specific communities.

In the past decade, an alternative view of literacy has emerged, one much more consonant with the intellectual foundations of writing groups. Supporters of this alternative take exception to the "great divide" theory of the technological/skill definition. They describe it as reductive, arguing that literacy takes a variety of forms and is highly culture-dependent. These revisionist scholars undercut claims for literacy's monolithic qualities and capacity for enhancing intellectual and social development with careful investigation of counter-examples. They point to instances where oral reading skill is not matched by comprehension of what is read (Johanson), where literacy in the absence of formal education does not lead to higher levels of cognition (Scribner and Cole), where the skills of reading and writing function very differently in adjacent communities (Brice-Heath), where literacy and textuality can be separated (Stock, Pattison), where literacy does not necessarily yield higher status to its possessors (Cressy, Graff).

This revisionist work in literacy studies assumes that literacy is a complex social phenomenon, that its precise definition varies with social context. Adherents to this "ideology" model, as Street terms it, claim that the nature, development, and use of literacy grows directly out of the immediate social environment. Harvey Graff, one of the earliest of the revisionists, concluded his examination of nineteenth-century literacy by claiming that "the meaning of literacy in mid-nineteenth century urban society can only be understood in context" (292). He went on to generalize his point: "Literacy, finally, can no longer be seen as a universalistic quantity or quality to be possessed however unequally by all in theory. . . . literacy must be accorded a new understanding—in social context. If its social meanings are to be understood and its value best utilized, the 'myth of literacy' must be exploded" (323-24). The myth to which Graff objects relies upon a technological/skill definition of literacy.

In keeping with Graff's assertions, a number of recent studies have examined the nature, development, and use of literacy in terms of the immediate social environment. They take what Brian Street terms an "ideological" view of literacy. Shirley Brice Heath's study of two Piedmont communities gives prominence to how child-rearing, religious practices, and recreational activities contributed to the contrasting manifestations of literacy evident in the adjacent communities of Roadville and Trackton. She notes that language use and instruction in Roadville support "a fixed set of roles and view of the world, and provide a continual test of commitment to existing modes and values of social institutions and relationships" (144) while in Trackton language is for "negotiation and manipulation—both serious and playful" (235). Accordingly, "For Roadville, the written word limits alternatives of expression; in Trackton, it opens alternatives" (235). Arguing against dichotomizing, Heath explains, "in terms of the usual distinctions made between oral and literate tradition, neither community may be simply classified as either 'oral' or 'literate'" (230). In undercutting the oral/literate dichotomy on which the technical/skills definition of literacy depends, Heath demonstrates the need for a more flexible definition, one that can accommodate the varying forms of literacy she has so eloquently chronicled.

Scribner and Cole's study of literacy among the Vai people of Africa shared with Heath's investigation a careful attention to details of development and use of literacy and arrived at similar conclusions about the inadequacy of the "myth of literacy." They found that in the absence of formal education literacy made little difference in intellectual processes and concluded that "there is no evidence in these data to support the construct of a general 'literacy' phenomenon. Although many writers discuss literacy and its social and psychological implications as though literacy entails the same knowledge and skills whenever people read or write, our experimental outcomes support our social analysis in demonstrating that literacies are highly differentiated" (132). Just as Heath calls the oral/literate dichotomy into question, so Scribner and Cole undermine claims of technical/skills literacy for the cognitive benefits of reading and writing. If literacy separated from formal education does not impart demonstrably enhanced capacities for abstract thought, then it cannot be described as the transportable skill that the technical definition implies.

Historical as well as contemporary examinations support the ideological view of literacy. David Cressy, a social historian who studied literacy in Tudor and Stuart England, found wide and unexpected variations among various subgroups in the population. Literacy developed most strongly where it was needed by people and failed to develop where it was not. Cressy observes: "Illiteracy is not a disease, to be eradicated like yellow fever, but rather it is a complex cultural condition linked to expectations and circumstances and rooted in the environment. . . . Literacy will flourish where those who are offered it are aware of and can experience its benefits" ("Environment" 41). Although he does not address them directly, Cressy could be speaking to literacy advocates such as Oxenham and Maheu who argue that skills of reading and writing should be spread as quickly and broadly as possible. In demonstrating that cultural contexts shape the needs and uses of literacy, Cressy shows the inherent fallacy of assuming that everyone needs literacy to the same degree.

Recent literacy studies not only reveal the weaknesses of the technical/skills definition, they also yield new, broader definitions of literacy. Brian Stock, drawing on his examination of literacy in the eleventh and twelfth centuries, claims: "Literacy is not textuality. One can be literate without the overt use of texts, and one can use texts extensively without evidencing genuine literacy" (7). For Stock, genuine literacy refers to culturally defined norms of learning, and in the medieval period these were frequently oral. Robert Pattison makes a related point about literacy in contemporary society by defining it as "consciousness of the questions posed by language coupled with mastery of those skills by which a culture at any given moment in its history manifests this consciousness" (5). According to Pattison, this consciousness need not involve skills of reading and writing, and he predicts that electronic media will propagate the "new literacy" of our society (205). The meaning of literacy thus extends from encoding and decoding written symbols to understanding meaning in a specific social context.

Studies operating under the ideological definition assume that literacy means joining a specific community through understanding the issues it considers important and developing the capacity to participate in conversations about those issues. As used here, the term *conversation* refers to Kenneth Bruffee's use of the word, the "conversation of mankind" that enables reflective thought and results from social engagement in intellectual pursuits. Mastery of skills such as reading and writing may be essential to joining a specific literate community, but while necessary, these skills are not sufficient because ability to encode and decode does not of itself guarantee anyone admission to a literate community. Some composition instructors who have tried to join a community of, say, physicists, know too well how inadequate reading and writing skills can be. Furthermore, as Elizabeth Eisenstein has noted, not all who master the written word become members of a book-reading community, a community in which members read to learn once they have learned to read. In other words, literacy defined in technological/skill terms does not suffice for membership in literate communities.

Writing groups, seen in terms of this broader definition that links literacy and community, take on large implications. If becoming literate means joining a community, and if literacy varies from one community to another, then complaints about "illiteracy" speak to the fact that individuals have not absorbed sufficiently the mores of a given community, whether that community be a college class or the more amorphous "American culture." This problem, one facing both educators and the larger society, cannot be addressed by moving "back to the basics" and placing a "greater emphasis . . . on reading, writing and arithmetic" (Fadiman and Howard 123). But it is a problem with particular urgency for English studies because, as E. D. Hirsch has noted, English has a unique nationalizing function in American education ("Formalism" 351). If citizens are to become members of intellectual and social communities beyond those into which they are born, they are likely to do so in English classes. Defining literacy as membership in a given community means identifying one of literacy's central purposes as prescribing the terms by which individuals enter certain communities. Accordingly, composition instructors, in particular, face the task of initiating students into communities of educated people. Indeed, Patricia Bizzell has argued that composition classes should introduce students into academic discourse communities and that "to neglect the context of writing and knowledge is to risk committing a new version of the social injustice attributable to the old composition course" (205). Bizzell refers to the social injustice of excluding some individuals from the literate community, usually an academic one, to which they seek entry.

Writing groups offer a means for individuals, both in and outside of school, to enter literate communities. The collaboration and language development inherent in writing groups insure that participants will begin to develop the cognitive abilities essential to literacy in the broad sense. In addition, evidence from studies of early literacy demonstrates that the processes by which children initially become literate have much in common with what occurs in writing groups.

Gumperz and Dyson, in their respective examinations of emergent literacy in young children, find that youngsters succeed in becoming literate to the extent that they learn to use language in new ways. Children in the early years of elementary school find occasions for broadening their repertoires of language use during the interaction of "sharing time." As they narrate events from their lives, children learn to develop a coherent oral text, to consider the perspectives of others, and to adjust their language accordingly. Similarly, the collaboration of writing groups offers participants of more advanced years opportunities to observe and practice new forms of language that they can internalize as part of their own language development.

Joining a community of any sort depends upon affective qualities as well as cognitive ones, and literate communities are no exception. Attitude plays a large part in individuals' ability and willingness to become literate or to participate in literate communities. Persons who have negative feelings about reading and writing are much less likely to participate in literate communities than individuals who feel positively disposed toward these activities. Stereotypical responses of "I'd better watch my language" or "I never did like to write" that greet English teachers in social situations indicate the degree to which negative attitudes toward literacy infect the general population, and these negative attitudes can lead individuals to exclude themselves from communities where literacy plays a significant role.

Powerful evidence of these negative attitudes takes the form of aliteracy. Aliterates do not lack technical skills, but because they have no sense of belonging to the literate community, they withdraw. Like Bartleby, they "prefer not to" read and write. Statistics on newspaper circulation provide one indication of this phenomenon. From 1970 to 1981 daily circulation of newspapers dropped 7 percent, the number of books published has dropped 5000 over the last several years, and teenagers do little reading for pleasure, preferring to spend time on movies and television (Thimmesch 3–4, 29, 37). Causes of aliteracy are difficult to define precisely, but at a recent symposium representatives of television, newspapers, magazines, education, and publishing companies speculated that the causes include teaching, which robs students of "some of the enjoyment in reading" (Thimmesch 4). Failure of community underlies this statement, for it is in community that individuals learn to enjoy reading and writing.

The losses incurred by aliteracy include "critical thinking skills, predicting skills and argumentation skills" and exercise of the voting franchise. Ultimately, aliteracy may lead to a two-class system of an educated elite and an aliterate majority (Thimmesch 18, 24). In such a situation, "if the gap between the educated minority and the undereducated mass becomes too great, the opportunities for political manipulation will grow" and the democratic system of government will be threatened (Thimmesch 39).

In many ways these claims echo Thomas Jefferson's famous statement about newspapers in a democracy: "Were it left to me to decide whether we should have a government without a newspaper, or newspapers without a government, I should not hesitate a moment to prefer the latter. But I should mean that every man should receive these papers and be capable of reading them." If we assume "receive" to include motivation in its meaning, then Jefferson's juxtaposition of "receive" and "be capable of reading" implies that a combination of skill and attitude is essential to membership in a literate community, and that reinforces the Thimmesch statement about the importance of literacy to democracy.

Becoming literate enough to be willing to participate in a democracy means becoming part of a community, and instructors need ways to help students into the literate community. Writing groups offer one way. Founders of college literary societies, of young men's associations, of women's clubs, and of other self-sponsored groups all understood, implicitly or explicitly, that literacy is a social activity and that the best way to become more literate was to join with others. Instructors who have established classroom writing groups likewise operated on the assumption that literacy thrives in a community. To be sure, the value of writing groups varies with the effectiveness of their functioning, and only those groups with adequate preparation, commitment, and clarity of task can ease students into a literate community. When writing groups work well, however, they enhance students' chances of joining the literate community of which that group is a part.

Historical origins point to the connection between writing groups and literate communities. As this book has shown, students and non-students initiated writing groups because they "knew" that literacy belongs to a community. One of the attributes most frequently credited to writing groups is a positive attitude. Variously expressed as motivation toward writing, a warmer classroom climate, and enthusiasm for revision, this positive attitude can counter the negativism that leads to aliteracy. Educational movements and specific historical events have come and gone, but the pervasive motivation toward creating communities of literacy has endured and prevailed. Differences of age, circumstance, and historical period disappear before this common motivation.

Finally, writing groups, as this book has shown, focus on the social dimension of writing, reminding participants that literacy does not function in isolation. In writing groups, people can become part of a community that takes aesthetic pleasure in a fine sentence, distinguishes between a convincing argument and one that fails to convince, and delights in clear and effective presentation of an idea. The product of writing groups, the polished prose, has importance, but even more significant is the process of the group, the means by which individuals experience and eventually become part of a literate community.

Bibliography

Part 1

Primary Sources on Writing Groups

The following is a chronological listing of books and articles about writing groups. It documents their history, as well as recommendations for and benefits assigned to these groups. (Full citations appear in part 2.) Over the years, support for writing groups has clustered around a few key ideas: participants produce higher-*quality* writing than their peers, who follow more traditional practices; participants develop more positive *attitudes* about writing, including increased motivation toward writing and revision of writing, reduced anxiety about writing, greater self-esteem, more sense of authority about their own texts, and enhanced feelings of solidarity with other writers; participants experience *intellectual* growth, including development of critical thinking skills, enhanced evaluative capacities, and greater ability to transfer learning from one task to another; and participants increase their *rhetorical* skill, particularly their ability to conceptualize and address the needs of their audience. Benefits for teachers include a more reasonable *paper load* because writing groups can reduce the number of papers a teacher must evaluate while enhancing the quality of writing that reaches the teacher's desk. Because of the reduced work load, teachers can effect *instructional* improvements, including more individualized attention for students and greater adherence to a naturalistic or process-oriented approach to writing. And some instructional comments focus on ways teachers can improve writing groups. To aid the reader in following the emergence and development of these various rationales, I have appended appropriate key words to each year in which publications about writing groups appeared.

1880: ATTITUDES
Lord: In response to an inquiry from a teacher interested in increasing student motivation toward writing, the author suggests that students read their writing aloud and criticize one another.

1892: PAPER LOAD
Wright: Includes recommendation that students "to some extent correct one another's written work" (22).

1894: INSTRUCTIONAL, INTELLECTUAL
Maxwell: Includes discussion of procedure whereby students exchange papers and "correct the mistakes of one another" (243).

1895: QUALITY, ATTITUDE, INSTRUCTIONAL, INTELLECTUAL, PAPER LOAD, RHETORICAL
Bright: Describes Johns Hopkins University course in which writing groups enable students to improve their work.
Cook: Composition courses at Yale include writing groups aimed at improving student work.
Dodge: Writing groups in literary societies do such an effective job that their products are accepted in required composition classes at the University of Illinois.
Frankenberger: Literary society writing groups are applauded for the quality of instruction they provide participants.
Genung: Composition classes at Amherst use the "laboratory" method which asks students to critique printed copies of one another's work.
MacLean: The English department at the University of Minnesota sees writing groups in literary societies as adjuncts to the department because of the high quality of instruction they provide.
Schelling: Composition classes at the University of Pennsylvania include oral readings of and group response to student papers.

1897: RHETORICAL
Thurber: Advocates that students read one another's work because audience response is the writer's reward.

1901: RHETORICAL, INSTRUCTIONAL
Buck: Urges more natural conditions for writing instruction, including student critiques based on questions such as "Did I succeed in reproducting my experience exactly in my friend's mind?" and "Did he see each event as it had passed before my eyes?" (380).

1902: ATTITUDE, RHETORICAL, INSTRUCTIONAL, QUALITY, INTELLECTUAL, PAPER LOAD
Valentine: Reports on 1901 composition class at MIT where students'

critiques of one another's work counted for half their grade. In addition to describing the procedures used and the benefits derived, the author includes a number of student themes with student comments attached.

1905: QUALITY, RHETORICAL
Carpenter: Text for common school students recommends writing groups as a means for improving clarity and coherence of compositions.

1905: INTELLECTUAL
Noyes: Recommends peer critiques because "examining others' work soon makes [students] sensitive to their own blunders" (699). Meets criticisms of this method with strategies for enabling students to be effective critics.

1906: RHETORICAL, INSTRUCTIONAL
Buck: Text for elementary school students recommends writing groups as a way to increase students' awareness of audience in writing.

1912: INTELLECTUAL, INSTRUCTIONAL
Tressler: Claims that student correction aids intellectual development and makes teaching more efficient.

1913: INSTRUCTIONAL
Robinson: Asserts that few successful teachers of composition use textbooks. Instead they employ practices such as conferences, "oral composition" and peer response.

1914: QUALITY, RHETORICAL
Cady: A "laboratory" course at Middlebury College uses writing groups to improve student writing.
Cooper: "It has been my experience that freshman and sophomores will study more and will prepare better compositions, when they must read their work aloud before a dozen of their fellows whom they have come to know as individuals, and in the presence of a teacher whom they know in an intimate way, than under any other external conditions" (295–96).

1916: RHETORICAL, INSTRUCTIONAL
Leonard: "Oral and written composition are developed in a socially organized class to carry out real projects and are criticized by the children themselves in a spirit of hearty co-operation" (509).

1917: INSTRUCTIONAL
Leonard: Text for common school students recommends that they participate in writing groups to improve their writing.

Walker: Small group work in composition classes allows for more individual attention to students and "the task of composition becomes a friendly competition" (449).

1918: RHETORICAL

Watt: The class can serve as an audience to "criticize the ideas of the paper" thereby making authors more conscious of their audience (160).

1919: ATTITUDES, QUALITY, INSTRUCTIONAL

Hedges: Recounts experience with college students who criticized one another's work as part of writing a play collaboratively.

Thompson: Peer response distinguishes socialized from academic method, and empirical study revealed that students taught by the socialized method wrote with fewer mechanical errors and learned faster than students taught by the academic method.

Ziegler: Describes a writing lab in which students criticize one another's writing regularly.

1920: INTELLECTUAL, ATTITUDES

Beverley: Urges that students learn to evaluate their own writing.

McKee: Students jointly edit papers for a collection on Shakespeare.

1923: QUALITY, INTELLECTUAL

Hatfield: Describes "the project method" which includes group criticism of student writing.

1925: QUALITY

Smith: Asserts that asking students to use their own resources will increase satisfactory writing.

Thie: Comparison of class using writing groups with class using regular methods demonstrated that students in writing groups wrote better than those in the regular class.

1926: RHETORICAL, QUALITY

Bright: Reports on survey of fifty schools and indicates that texts and practices are changing to more socialized approach. Benefits of writing groups include: "promotes intelligent democracy" (366) and "the pupil has the benefit of different viewpoints" (367).

1929: QUALITY, RHETORICAL, INTELLECTUAL

Horner: Compares lab and regular methods and finds lab better. Concludes: "In the teaching of English composition, pupil direction in study is of fundamental importance" (221).

Morris: Students in a small school criticize one another's writing and benefit from "the creation of a critical attitude" (31).

1930: ATTITUDE, RHETORICAL, INSTRUCTIONAL,
INTELLECTUAL
Crawford and Phelan: Seventeen variations on student mutual correction exist but all "cultivate a social spirit or atmosphere in the
room which will make individual pupils willing to take criticism
kindly from their fellow students" (619).
Roberts: Urges writing club as best means to develop sense of audience and asserts: "Student writers must be led to accept faculty
judgment in art as valuable but no more significant than their own"
(752).
Wheeler: Describes a Johns Hopkins University lab course where
students read and criticize one another's work.

1932: ATTITUDE
Debbs: Teacher brings own writing to be read and criticized in class
along with everyone else's.

1933: QUALITY, RHETORICAL
Johnson: Comparison of regular and experimental classes (which
included writing groups) revealed that students in experimental
classes wrote better.
Ward: The writing group's "real purpose is to furnish an audience for
those who have original work to read" (292).

1937: INSTRUCTIONAL, ATTITUDE, QUALITY
Forster: Describes a college writing lab characterized by self-directed
work where students "discuss problems with others" (733).
Gallagher: A lack of student ability and motivation led to organizing
the class into small groups featuring "group criticism" where "compositions were torn apart and rebuilt" (562).

1939: INSTRUCTIONAL
Munz: Use of the dileascope enables whole-class criticism of student
writing.

1940: RHETORICAL, QUALITY
Buckner: Describes students who write a book on college life with
each student responsible for one chapter. "These [chapters] were
criticized by the classes and the instructor, [and] returned for revision . . ." (280).
Eberhart: Urges teachers so see composition as a social act requiring
"frequent opportunity for writing to be read aloud [for] group
evaluation" (392).

130   Bibliography

1945: ATTITUDE, INTELLECTUAL
Buckley: Emphasizes importance of free expression of ideas in America and gives special attention to writing groups.
Newland: A high school lab includes presentation and discussion of student papers on a variety of topics.

1946: QUALITY
LaBrant: To get honest writing, a teacher must encourage "responsible writing," and this is achieved by reading student writing aloud and discussing it.

1947: PAPER LOAD, INTELLECTUAL
Bernardette: Advocates that students correct papers and claims that they will benefit as much as the teacher whose paper load is reduced.

1950: QUALITY, INTELLECTUAL, RHETORICAL
Drake: The process of developmental writing includes a "partner conference" wherein two students meet and "get a reader into the act" (4).
Hayakawa: Recommends that "students in freshman English write not for the teacher but for each other . . . the merits of a theme should be judged not by the teacher but by classmates with the teacher acting only as chairman" (99). "I should go so far as to recommend that the grading be done by students" (102).
Leek: Small group editing improves the quality of student writing.
Paul: Groups of students select the best paper written by a group member and these papers are scrutinized in a whole-class competition.

1951: QUALITY, RHETORICAL, PAPER LOAD
Macrorie: Students should read one another's papers to the class because the reader learns to speak better and the writer can tell from stumbles what isn't clear.
Maize: Crowded classes lead to peer review of writing, but this practice merely supplements and does not replace other forms of instruction. Composition partners provide one another a "suitable audience" (399).

1952: ATTITUDE, INTELLECTUAL, RHETORICAL
Gelshenen: A judicial mode of peer evaluation motivates more and better writing.
Kostick: Advocates that students respond to one another's writing (in writing). Then the teacher grades the work and student critics can compare their responses to the teacher's.

Lawson: Students bring samples of their own writing for paragraph study and select best papers for class reading.

Sorenson: Among the new methods cited is this: "Themes are not written for the teacher; they are written for the class" (161).

1954: QUALITY, ATTITUDE, RHETORICAL

Maize: Describes an experimental lab course where "analysis and comment were provided . . . by fellow students" (46), and these students wrote better than those in regular classes."

Report of Workshop: Speakers at national convention suggest that one way to move from reading to writing is through analysis of student writing because "frequently criticism from peers is much more effective than that by teachers" (129).

1955: INTELLECTUAL, RHETORICAL

Gregory: Students read papers to small groups and select the best for class reading. Criteria for judging include interest, clarity, and sentence structure.

LaBrant: Writers deserve response and student papers "should be read to the class" where criticism means discussion of ideas, and suggestions come from lack of clarity (74).

1956: INSTRUCTIONAL, INTELLECTUAL, PAPER LOAD

Laird: When small groups of students grade one another's papers they receive more instruction in writing, and the instructor notes, "my job was no longer mainly criticizing students' work but showing students how to criticize one another's and their own work" (134).

Livingston: Describes how whole classes respond critically to mimeo copies of student papers.

Report of Workshop: Speakers at national convention suggest that overburdened instructors use "student critics of student themes" (169).

1957: INTELLECTUAL

Dusel: Refers to the 1956 volume by the Commission on English Curriculum and its recommendation of peer evaluation. Affirms value of giving students "lots of practice in discriminating quality in writing on their own level of achievement" (267).

1959: INTELLECTUAL, RHETORICAL

Grisson: Students' independent evaluation of composition is a goal of the composition class, and students therefore need small group work on evaluation.

Hausdorff: After a student has written a report "an audience is readily available: his own class" (29).

1961: INSTRUCTIONAL, ATTITUDE, INTELLECTUAL
Mersand: "Composition correction has changed from a pursuit in red ink by a bleary-eyed teacher-detective to a constructive evaluation which is shared in by the student-writer and the class" (235).

1962: ATTITUDE, INTELLECTUAL, PAPER LOAD
Ashmead: Two weeks of composition class discussions recorded by instructor and rechecked with students included small group peer tutorials on writing.
Cozzo: To motivate writing, Saturday writing clinics are held where small groups read and analyze students' writing, and some good papers are ultimately published.
Johnson: Describes a method of organizing a class into small peer review groups that have directives on what to listen for as students read their papers. "This system of small group evaluation renders it unnecessary for the teacher to mark some sets of papers at all" (491).

1963: INTELLECTUAL, RHETORICAL
Brown: Argues that learning to write well requires practice and a critical audience. Accordingly students should learn to become critics of their own writing.
Salerno: Describes a class whose work includes "pooling of the knowledge of the group by exchanging papers for student corrections and comments on a bi-weekly basis" (39).

1964: INSTRUCTIONAL, INTELLECTUAL, RHETORICAL
Blackman: Recommends peer evaluation and urges firm teacher control and discontinuation at the first sign that "participants are losing a sense of objectivity" (32).
Douglas: Subdivisions of a large class use "do it yourself criticism sessions" (124) where students respond to one another's work.

1965: INTELLECTUAL
Bernadette: Student writing is read aloud in lab session and evaluated in light of "listening, criticism, discussion and individual decision" (24), and this student involvement leads to "independent, mature thinking and writing" (23).

1966: INTELLECTUAL
Lindsay: A combination of individual conferences and writing groups replace regular class meetings so students can develop their own criteria for excellence in writing.

1967: RHETORICAL, ATTITUDE, QUALITY
Greenbaum: Describes engineering students who do group projects which include editing their own writing in small groups.
Stewart: Engaging students in revision is the composition teacher's most important task, and writing groups can accomplish it.
Tovatt and Miller: Includes small group critiques as part of study of oral-aural-visual procedures in teaching writing. Investigation of OAV method was inconclusive but generally positive.

1968: INTELLECTUAL, QUALITY, RHETORICAL, ATTITUDE
Burnett: Describes college writing program that includes peer review.
Elbow: Calls on Aristotle, Cicero and Quintilian for value of transaction between writer and audience. To this end recommends that students "all get copies [of papers] and judge their effectiveness" (117).
Macroric (a): Advocates that students read their work aloud to one another in order to eliminate phony or artificial diction from their writing.
Macrorie (b): Students read work aloud and receive criticism from peers rather than participate in teacher-dominated conference because peer method has advantage of "providing praise from fellow students" (692).
Moffett: Portrays writing groups as integral to the decentering and audience awareness essential to mature writing.
Murray: Describes physical layout of a classroom where writing groups can work.

1969: QUALITY, RHETORICAL, INTELLECTUAL, ATTITUDE
Macrorie: Recommends freshman writing seminar in which "each student reads his paper aloud" and receives criticism from the class.
Murray: A curriculum to help students meet responsibilities of free speech should include having the "class read each other's papers in small groups" (120).
Stade: Urges writing groups, claiming: "As critics of each other's work, the students tend to be more generous in their praise, more severe in their adverse judgments, more patient, and more courteous, than their teacher is likely to be" (155).
Wolf: Cites advantages of small group discussion for learning to write.
Zoellner: "One of the most important characteristics of the talk-write classroom is that it makes writing and the analysis and criticism of writing a *Social Event*" (301).

1970: INTELLECTUAL, ATTITUDE, RHETORICAL,
INSTRUCTIONAL QUALITY

Bellas: Small group critique of writing is well received by students, and benefits include reduced inhibitions, greater motivation, more responsibility, and increased ability to use language.

Erickson: Methods class uses face-to-face response to writing to train prospective teachers.

Hamalion: Students read their work aloud to the class and receive indications of whether their aims have been achieved. "The class becomes the critic."

Judy: Advocates naturalistic approach which includes "time for reading and sharing of completed pieces" (217) because "students probably constitute their own best audience" (216).

Putz: Describes experimental use of writing groups in college classes and notes their advantages.

Strong: Urges that writing classes include group critique because "a young writer can learn a great deal from what his contemporaries say about his work; furthermore he is more likely to take it to heart" (811).

Strout: Discusses a workshop that includes peer review:
"As students read and evaluate each other's essays, they learn to become diagnosticians" (1130).

1971: ATTITUDE, INTELLECTUAL, RHETORICAL, QUALITY

Elbow: Examines own practices and claims: "The best thing about my course is the fact that each student writes something weekly he knows the rest of the class will read, and for the most part, comment on" (745).

Karrfalt: Asserts that in writing groups students "experienced a situation for writing that was essentially *social* as opposed to *individual*, thus giving an added importance to the *communication* phase of writing" (378).

Kaufman: Claims that teachers should give student more freedom, including "encouraging students to say exactly what they understand in another's work" (386) and to suggest revisions.

Snipes: Enumerates advantages of peer response as including independent thought, ease in understanding, shared responsibility, exposure to a wide audience, practice in evaluation, and writing for an audience. Disadvantages include lack of teacher stimulation and motivation, domination by the same student, and lack of preparation by some students.

1972: RHETORICAL, INTELLECTUAL, PAPER LOAD
  Bruffee: Traces theoretical background of collaborative learning and advocates writing groups because they enable students to understand more fully the nature of knowledge, the human mind, and the experience of learning.
  Hipple: Suggestions for reducing the teacher's paper load include having students comment on one another's writing. A side benefit is a wider audience for student writers.
  Jarabeck and Dieterich: Lists writing groups among new options for evaluation of student writing.
  Wilcox: Describes college composition class where "papers are mimeographed and discussed in class" (696).

1973: QUALITY, ATTITUDE, RHETORICAL, INSTRUCTIONAL
  Bennett: Describes class where students write on topics of interest to them and respond to one another's writing. "We are not interested in what he meant to say, only what is on the paper" (584).
  Bruffee: Claims that students learn more and write better as a result of peer response.
  Elbow: Advocates teacherless writing groups in which participants offer one another direct response to writing in progress.
  Glatthorn: Advocates writing groups as a way of enhancing cooperation and creativity among students.
  Judy: Evaluation should resemble editorial work and should include "asking students to share writing with each other and to suggest how papers can be revised to be more effective with the audience" (77).
  Kelly: Describes an "open class" wherein students respond to one another's work and become more competent and creative writers.
  Lagana: Study of writing groups revealed that students who participated wrote better and were less anxious about their writing.
  McNamara: Advocates writing groups for their effectiveness in editing.
  Pumphrey: Urges a shift away from teacher-student evaluation to student-peer evaluation of writing.
  Snipes: Describes talk, write, talk, write process which includes reading work to peers to get suggestions for improvement.
  Welch: Class cohesiveness, achieved by hearing and responding to one another's work, leads to increased motivation among students.

1974: QUALITY, PAPER LOAD
  Graber: Systematic examination of "teacherless" class reveals that students' writing does improve.

Hardaway: Claims that writing groups can lighten the teacher's paper load.

1975: ATTITUDE, RHETORICAL, QUALITY, INTELLECTUAL, PAPER LOAD, INSTRUCTIONAL

Bouton and Tutty: An experimental study revealed that students in writing groups improved their writing more than students in a traditional class.

Clark: Recommends "the constant informal swapping of papers" (68) as a means of individualizing a writing program.

Ellman: Writing group participation "sharpens the critical skills of the evaluators and provides immediate and palatable feedback for those being evaluated" (79).

Kuykendall: Advocates "naturalistic" teaching where "students meet in small groups to comment on one another's papers" (6–7).

Rizzo: Peer teaching increases attention and interest in class as well as student self-esteem.

Shuman: Revision works best through peer response because "one's peers would constitute a rather good audience" (42).

Steward: Motivation toward writing increases as students work in a lab that includes writing groups in its work.

Wagner: Teachers can justify reducing their paper load by using writing groups because "students can learn a great deal from one another" (78).

1976: QUALITY, ATTITUDE, RHETORICAL, INSTRUCTIONAL, PAPER LOAD, INTELLECTUAL

Beach: Writing groups foster intellectual growth because participants translate peer evaluation into their own concepts for revising.

Brosnaham: Responding to student compositions in writing groups frees the teacher from correcting everything.

Cooper et al.: Describes new middle school program that includes peer response based on Elbow model. Students "can respond to each other's writings in helpful ways" (59). They don't grade but "describe for each other how they perceive particular pieces" (60).

Hawkins: Advocates workshop procedures that include spoken and written peer responses, and in which instructor sometimes gives specific tasks.

Higley: Parodies a nonfunctioning writing group to illustrate potential problems.

Leonard: Advocates "Tryworks," which are read for writing groups and "give students the sense of audience every writer needs" (62).

Macrorie: Repeats text's first edition advocacy of writing groups.

Megna: Describes the SEG (sensitivity, exposure, grading) system, which builds trust among students, shows them criteria for evaluation, and asks them to use the criteria.

Messelaar: Writing groups can use teacher-provided scales to evaluate one another's work.

1977: ATTITUDE, INTELLECTUAL, QUALITY, RHETORICAL

Beaven: Peer evaluation in writing groups enhances motivation toward writing and increases positive feelings among students.

Gebhardt (a): The training of writing teachers should include attention to "students as their own editors and teachers" (139).

Gebhardt (b): Among strategies suggested is drawing on group resources by asking students to read drafts and suggest material "writers could use as they continue drafting" (32).

Rothman: Advocates writing groups as a means of addressing literacy problems.

Walsh: Learning to write letters of application can be enhanced by using writing groups that discuss evolving letters.

Wixon: Adapts Zoellner's talk-write strategies to middle school so students use each other's strengths and the students provide "an audience for the writer" (72).

1978: ATTITUDE, INSTRUCTIONAL, INTELLECTUAL, RHETORICAL.

Beck et al.: Writing labs can and should provide a place where students can critique one another's work.

Bruffee: Claims that writing groups promote intellectual growth and develop critical judgment.

Denman: Strategies to reduce anxiety and increase affiliation and success in composition classes include writing groups.

Dilworth and Reising: Recognizing the social and moral dimensions of writing leads naturally to writing groups.

Harris: Writing groups provide the continuing feedback necessary to developing writing abilities.

Hill: Students need an "audience with whom they can share not only their ideas and individual thinking habits but also their mistakes" (893).

Jacko: Assigned roles of reader, writer and observer lead to more effective writing groups than do unstructured groups.

Moore: Advocates writing in composition class and uses considerable peer response to foster it.

Peckham: After instituting classroom writing groups as a result of NWP participation this teacher claims to be more effective because "students value their peer's opinions more than a teacher's" (62).

1979: INTELLECTUAL, RHETORICAL, QUALITY

Bean: Students who are given careful instructions for evaluating writing begin to understand that writing "can be judged by objective standards" (302).

Crowhurst: Examination of students' responses in writing groups revealed three categories of comments: encouragment, comments on content, and suggestions for improvement.

Falk: Cites Moffett on need for audience response and argues that writers need an audience (like that provided by a writing group) just as those acquiring a language do.

Maimon: Reading and responding to the writing of their classmates can help writers overcome egocentrism in their work and give more attention to their audience.

1980: ATTITUDE, RHETORICAL, INSTRUCTIONAL, INTELLECTUAL

Bruffee: Recommends writing groups to train peer tutors to distinguish descriptive, evaluative, and substantive comments.

Fox: Empirical investigation shows that writing groups reduce writing apprehension.

Gebhardt: Argues that peer feedback reduces the emotional isolation of writing.

Hawkins: Writing groups link writers and audiences because they help create the social structures that enable students to rehearse life as an "insider" in college writing.

Hammer: Among seven "rules" for composition is one asserting that teachers should "Expand the concept of audience by having the students read their work to one another" (49).

Healy: Preparation for writing groups includes whole-class response and model groups; audio and video tapes can help teacher monitor groups; course grades should reflect students' contributions to writing groups.

Hogan: Applying coaching techniques to writing instruction includes establishing writing groups in which "members instruct each other" (24).

Kirby: A peer audience gives students a reason to revise and "students need to hear their writing" (45).

Lamberg: Benefits of writing groups include "multiple and varied audience" and development of "critical reading skills" (68).

Peckham: Students in writing groups revise more because "students may ignore teachers, but they want to impress their friends" (52).

Podis: Students who participate in writing groups need to understand various teaching styles, need knowledge about language, and need to develop interpersonal skills.

Ylvisaker: Describes ideal class wherein students read their work aloud, listen to critiques and ask "How does this sound?" (74).

1981: QUALITY, INTELLECTUAL, ATTITUDE, RHETORICAL, INSTRUCTIONAL

Carroll: Argues that writers need talk as well as silence and recognizes four types: *Alchemistic* to aid prewriting; *Analytic* to shape a topic; *Evaluative* to aid revision; and *Closure* to deal with graded writing.

Clifford: Students taught with writing groups made significantly greater gains on a holistically scored writing sample than did students in traditional classes.

Fisher: Considers advantages and disadvantages of writing groups.

Fox: Claims that writing groups can work to make students better copy editors.

Fulweiler: Students learn to "show not tell" in writing groups. Describes critique sheets to be used by students.

Hipple: Teachers can reduce their paper load by employing writing groups.

James: Writing groups may not be new, but they are novel for this author. Teachers can use them to lighten the paper load without guilt because peer response has benefits of a real audience, motivation, aural response for students, development of critical sense, and growth of trust and independence in students.

Kelly: Addresses cynical high school teachers and urges connection of writing and learning, including writing groups, "to give them [students] a wider audience and other responses to their writing" (27).

Lapidus-Saltz: Urges that writer, not reader, be most active participant in writing group to ensure that insights from discussions are transferred to writing.

Lyons: Recommends that writing groups follow a three-part response including: "praise, question, and polish" (42).

Mason: Participating in the NWP, where she exchanged "personal writing with peers," revitalized the author and led her to use writing groups in her own class.

Myers: Examines aspects of voice as they appear in a writing group session.

Sears: Advises colleagues to provide a variety of audiences for student writers, and recommends writing groups for the audience they provide.

1982: ATTITUDE, INTELLECTUAL, RHETORICAL, QUALITY
Brannon and Knoblauch: Claims that students' authority over their own texts is frequently diminished by teachers, but writing groups can restore much of that authority by highlighting the intentions of student writers.
Ehrenberg: Advocates writing groups because they lead to productive work and encourage "student control and decision making" (65) in editing.
Gersten: "The most effective approach to getting students to take writing seriously is not teacher directed but student determined" (66), and this includes writing groups.
Liftig: Asserts that the basics movement has equated writing with correctness, resulting in aliteracy or the inability to have an aesthetic experience with an extended piece of language. A class survey revealed that no student had ever participated in a writing group or heard writing read aloud in class.
Lynch: Writing groups can use an analytic scale to sharpen critical awareness and develop a sense of personal accountability.
Peterson: Draws on work of Britton, Flower, Bleich, and Rosenblatt to argue that writing should be personal, and advocates writing groups to help revise such writing.
White: Recommends that students participate in holistic scoring of one another's writing to develop an understanding of what is expected in an essay.

1983: PAPER LOAD, INSTRUCTIONAL, RHETORICAL, INTELLECTUAL
Calkins: Elementary school writing workshop includes writing groups for which students are prepared by mini-lessons and conferences with the teacher. See pages 125–230.
Cantwell: Questions popular wisdom that writing groups can help reduce paper load by noting that students may not be motivated and may all need help at once.
Graves: Writing groups are based on four premises: children need to be aware of what helps; children need to be aware of what they know; new helping roles need to be introduced; children need increased access to each other.
Held: Writing groups grow out of a process approach to writing. They put time pressures on classes and should therefore be used in the

lab. Among benefits is the fact that a peer audience is less threatening than a teacher audience.

Kail: Claims that writing groups don't fit the linear model of education (teacher-teaches-student) because their activities are more circular and recursive.

MacLean: Students accustomed to writing groups comment on their own writing, confirming that "students not only can but do make judgments when they write" (66).

Rubin: Students don't always transfer learning from peer response to their own writing and need help with this transfer.

1984: ATTITUDE, INSTRUCTIONAL, INTELLECTUAL, RHETORICAL, INSTRUCTIONAL

Berkenkotter: Acknowledges that writing groups offer support, nonthreatening response, and additional perspectives, but argues that they may interfere with writers' authority over their texts.

Bruffee: Connects writing groups with post Cartesian philosophy and argues that experience in writing groups helps initiate students to the interpretive communities in which academic discourse is carried out.

Dyson: Documents the importance of writing groups to primary school writers.

Frantzen and Podis: Writing groups enable instructors to provide students individual attention without becoming exhausted.

George: Analyzes writing groups by categorizing them as task oriented, leaderless, and dysfunctional and suggests strategies for dealing with each.

Hilgers: Analysis of writing group language yields four categories: (1) feelings aroused by the text, (2) responses to surface features, (3) responses to the text as understood, and (4) responses to craftsmanship.

Jaech: Describes implementation of classroom writing groups and cites benefits of student motivation and improved writing.

Kelly et al.: Discusses methods of establishing writing groups in order to make them into effective writing teams.

Macrorie: Continues advocacy for writing groups or "helping circles" described in earlier editions.

Marcus: Writing groups provide nonjudgmental peers, thereby improving attitudes toward writing, enlarging the sense of audience, and making students responsible for technical aspects of writing.

NCTE Commission on Composition: Recommends, among other things, that "students should be encouraged to comment on each other's writing" (613).

Newkirk (a): Reports investigation of writing groups that revealed that students and instructors use different criteria in judging writing.

Newkirk (b): Protocol analysis of evaluations of teachers and students in writing groups reveals that students and teachers belong to different interpretive communities.

North: Advocates writing groups because intervention in the solitary act of writing through talk among peers helps break the old rhythms of writing.

Schuster: Recommends writing groups for college students because they integrate reading, writing, speaking, and listening; foster editing; and create a dialogic between writer and audience.

Strang: Suggests that the author, not the teacher, set the agenda for writing group evaluation.

Tsujimato: Revision is the most difficult part of teaching writing, and productive strategies include partner revision and writing groups.

1985: INTELLECTUAL, RHETORICAL, ATTITUDE, QUALITY

Atwell: Writing groups, a regular part of the elementary school class described here, are a source of ideas for writing.

Bruffee: This college composition text places writing groups at the center of a course designed to initiate students into an academic discourse community.

Clifton: Describes procedures for having students develop and use evaluative criteria to assign grades in writing groups.

Colasurdo: When students in writing groups work on publications, they edit seriously because their work is going into print.

Dyson: Children's classroom social life, including writing groups, contributes to their understanding of and capacity for literacy.

Gere (a): Examination of the language of writing groups reveals dominant informative and directive functions with variation according to type of writing.

Gere (b): Student comments in writing groups reveal more attention to specifics of texts than do typical teacher comments.

Murray: Suggests that teachers use writing groups to help students gauge the effectiveness of their work.

O'Donnell: Reports on a study that showed that students who participated in writing groups improved the communicative qualities of their written instructions.

Reither: Initiation into the academic world is best accompanied by workshop classes in which students read and write "for themselves and for each other."

Rouse: Demonstrates that writing groups can enable basic writers to improve their work.

Trimbur: Traces intellectual roots and implications of the collaborative learning essential to writing groups.

Part 2

List of Works Consulted

Abel, Elizabeth, ed. *American Accent: Fourteen Stories by Authors Associated with the Bread Loaf Writers' Conference.* New York: Ballantine, 1954.

Abrams, M. H. *The Mirror and the Lamp: Romantic Theory and the Critical Tradition.* New York: Oxford, 1953.

Anthony, Julia. "How a Club Paper Was Written." *Chautauquan* 32 (1900): 30–32.

Applebee, Arthur, with Anne Auten and Fran Lehr. *Writing in the Secondary Schools* Urbana: NCTE, 1981.

Ashmead, John. "The Life of a Composition Class." *College Composition and Communication* 13 (Dec. 1962): 20–25.

Atwell, Nancy. "Everyone Sits at a Big Desk: Discovering Topics for Writing." *English Journal* 74 (Sept. 1985): 35–39.

Aubry, John. "Fraternities, Literary Societies and Student Life at the University of Michigan 1845–1855." Unpublished essay, 1980, Michigan Historical Collections, Bentley Historical Library, University of Michigan.

Bakhtin, Mikhail [V.S. Volosinov]. *Marxism and the Philosophy of Language.* Trans. Ladislav Matejak and Ivan R. Titunik. New York: Studies in Language, 1973.

Bakhtin, Mikhail. *The Dialogic Imagination.* Trans. Caryl Emerson and Michael Holquist. Austin: U of Texas P, 1981.

Barnes, Douglas. "Language in the Secondary Classroom." *Language, the Learner and the School.* Harmondsworth: Penguin, 1971–77.

Barnes, Douglas, and Frankie Todd. *Communication and Learning in Small Groups.* London: Routledge, 1977.

Beach, Richard. "Self-Evaluationn Strategies of Extensive Revisers and Nonrevisers." *College Composition and Comunication* 27 (1976): 160–70.

Bean, John. "A Method of Peer-Evaluation of Student Writing." *College Composition and Communication* 30 (1979): 301–2.

Beaven, Mary. "Individualized Goal-Setting Self-Evaluation, and Peer Evaluation." *Evaluating Writing: Describing, Measuring, Judging.* Ed. Charles Cooper and Lee Odell. Urbana: NCTE, 1977. 135–56.

Beck, Paula, Thom Hawkins, and Marcia Silver. "Training and Using Peer Tutors." *College English* 40 (1978): 432–49.

Bellack, Arno A., Herbert M. Kliebard, Ronald T. Hyman, and Frank L. Smith. *The Language of the Classroom.* New York: Teachers College, 1966.

Bellas, Ralph. "Workshop Sessions in English Composition." *College Composition and Communication* 21 (1970): 271–73.

Bennett, John H. "Writing and My One Little Postage Stamp of Natural Soil." *English Journal* 61 (May 1972): 690–93.

Berkenkotter, Carol. "Student Writers and Their Sense of Authority over Texts." *College Composition and Communication* 35 (1984): 312–19.

Bernardette, Doris. "A Practical Proposal to Take the Drudgery out of the Teaching of Freshman Composition and to Restore to the Teacher His Pristine Measure in Teaching." *College English* 8 (1947): 383.

Bernadette, Sr. Miriam. "Evaluation of Writing: A Three-Part Program" *English Journal* 54 (1965): 23–27.

Beverly, Clara. "Self-Measurement by Elementary-School Pupils." *English Journal* 9 (1920): 331–37.

Bizzell, Patricia. "College Composition: Initiation into the Academic Discourse Community." *Curriculum Inquiry* 12 (1982): 191–207.

Blackman, Ralph. "Accentuate the Positive and Save the Red Pencil." *English Journal* 53 (1964): 31–33.

Blair, Karen. *The Clubwoman as Feminist: True Womanhood Redefined, 1868–1914.* New York: Holmes & Meier, 1980.

Bode, Carl. *The American Lyceum: Town Meeting of the Mind.* New York: Oxford UP, 1956.

Boorstin, Daniel. *The Americans: The Colonial Experience.* New York: Random House, 1958.

Bouton, Kathleen, and Gary Tutty. "The Effects of Peer-Evaluated Compositions on Writing Improvement." *The English Record* 26 (1975): 64–67.

Bowker, Richard R. *Copyright: Its History and Its Law.* Boston: Houghton Mifflin, 1912.

Brannon, Lil, and C. H. Knoblauch. "On Students' Rights to Their Own Texts: A Model of Teacher Response." *College Composition and Communication* 33 (1982): 157–66.

Brice-Heath, Shirley. *Ways with Words*. Cambridge: Cambridge UP, 1983.

Bright, M. Aline. "Pupil Participation in Theme Correction." *English Journal* 15 (1926): 358–67.

Bright, James. "English at the the Johns Hopkins University." *English in American Universities*. Ed. William Payne. Boston: Heath, 1895. 149–54.

Britton, James, Tony Burgess, Nancy Martin, Alex McLeod, and Harold Rosen. *The Development of Writing Abilities (11–18)*. London: Macmillan, 1977.

Brosnaham, Leger. "Getting Freshman Composition All Together." *College English* 37 (1976): 657–60.

Brown, Maurice. "Creating a Critical Audience." *College Composition and Communication* 14 (Dec. 1963): 263–64.

Bruffee, Kenneth. "The Way Out. A Critical Survey of Innovations in College Teaching with Special Reference to the December, 1971 Issue of *College English*." *College English* 33 (1972): 457–70.

———. "The Brooklyn Plan: Attaining Intellectual Growth through Peer-Group Tutoring." *Liberal Education* 64 (1978): 447-68.

———. "Collaborative Learning: Some Practical Models." *College English* 34 (1973): 579–86.

———. *Short Course in Writing*. 1980. Boston: Little, 1985.

———. "Collaborative Learning and the 'Conversation of Mankind.'" *College English* 46 (1984): 635–52.

Bruner, Jerome S. "The Social Context of Language Acquisition." *Language and Communication* 1 (1981): 155–78.

Buck, Gertrude. "Recent Tendencies in the Teaching of English Composition." *Educational Review* 22 (1901): 371–82.

Buck, Gertrude, and Elisabeth Woodbridge. *A Course in Expository Writing*. New York: Holt, 1906.

Buckley, Jerome H., and Paul L. Wiley. "The Technique of the Round Table in College Composition." *College English* 6 (1945): 411–12.

Buckner, Mabel A. "English Composition in Practice." *College English* 2 (1940): 279–81.

Burnett, Ronald. "Tutorial Composition." *College Composition and Communication* 18 (Dec. 1968): 255–58.

Cady, Frank. *A Freshman Course in English*. Middlebury: Middlebury College, 1914.

Calhoun, Daniel. *The Intelligence of a People*. Princeton: Princeton UP, 1973.

Calkins, Lucy McCormick. *Lessons from a Child*. Exeter: Heinemann, 1983.

Cantwell, Joan. "In the Ointments, A Few Flies." *English Journal* 72 (Dec. 1983): 55–56.

Carlyle, Thomas. *Past and Present*. 1843. New York: Burt, 1893.

Carmean, Stephen, and Morton Weir. "Effects of Verbalization on Discrimination, Learning and Retention." *Journal of Verbal Learning and Verbal Behavior* 6 (1967): 545–50.

Carpenter, George. *Elements of Rhetoric and Composition*. New York: Macmillan, 1902.

Carroll, Joyce Armstrong. "Talking through the Writing Process." *English Journal* 70 (Nov. 1981): 100–102.

Chase, Elizabeth Buffum, and Lucy Buffum Lowell. *Two Quaker Sisters*. New York: Liveright, 1937.

Cippola, Carlo. *Literacy and Development in the West*. London: Pelican, 1969.

Clanchy, Michael. *From Memory to Written Record*: England, 1066–1307. Cambridge: Harvard UP, 1979.

Clark, William. "How to Completely Individualize a Writing Program." *English Journal* 64 (Apr. 1975): 66–69.

Classic Culture Club. Yearbook, 1899. Northwest Collection, Suzallo Library, University of Washington.

Clifford, John "Composing in Stages: The Effects of a Collaborative Pedagogy." *Research in the Teaching of English* 15 (1981): 37–53.

Clifton, Linda. "What If the Kids Did It?" *Washington English Journal* 7 (Winter 1985): 12–16.

Coe, Edward. "The Literary Societies." *Yale College: A Sketch of Its History*. Ed. William Kingsley. New York: Holt, 1879. 307–23.

Colasurdo, Anthony. "The Literary Magazine as Class Project." *English Journal* 74 (Feb. 1985): 82–84.

Commager, Henry Steele. *The American Mind: An Interpretation of American Thought and Character Since the 1880's*. New Haven: Yale UP, 1950

Condon, W. S., and L. W. Sander. "Neonate Movement Is Synchronized with Adult Speech: Interactional Participation and Language Acquisition." *Science* (1974): 99–101.

Cook, Albert. "English at Yale University." *English in American Universities*. Ed. William Payne. Boston: Heath, 1895. 29–39.

Cooper, Charles, with Nancie M. Atwell, Denise L. David, Rita C. Giglia, William J. Grabe, and Carol P. Locke. "Tonawanda Middle Schools' New Writing Program." *English Journal* 65 (Nov. 1976): 56–61.

Cooper, Lane. "The Correction of Papers." *English Journal* 3 (1914): 290–98.

Cowley, Malcolm, ed. *Writers at Work: The Paris Review Interviews.* Harmondsworth: Penguin, 1958.

Cozzo, Joyce R. "Clinics for Writing." *English Journal* 51 (1962): 26–32.

Crawford, C. C., and Marie Phelan. "A Summary of Methods in Composition Work." *English Journal* 19 (1930): 615–30.

Cressy, David. *Literacy and the Social Order: Reading and Writing in Tudor and Stuart England.* Cambridge: Cambridge UP, 1980.

———. "The Environment for Literacy: Accomplishment and Context in Seventeenth-Century England and New England." *Literacy in Historical Perspective.* Ed. Daniel Resnick. Washington: Library of Congress, 1983. 23–42.

Croly, Jane Cunningham. *The History of the Woman's Club Movement in America.* New York: Allen, 1898.

Crowhurst, Marion. "The Writing Workshop: An Experiment in Peer Response to Writing." *Language Arts* 56 (1979): 757–62.

Cuban, Larry. *How Teachers Taught: Constancy and Change in American Classrooms 1890–1980.* New York: Longman, 1984.

Cubeta, Paul. Letter to the author. 17 August 1984.

Cutting, George. *Student Life at Amherst.* Amherst: Hatch & Williams, 1871.

Davis, Barbara Gross, Michael Scriven, and Susan Thomas. *The Evaluation of Composition Instruction.* Inverness, CA: Edgepress, 1981.

Debbs, J. McBride. "Freshman Special." *English Journal* 21 (1932): 743–50.

Denman, Mary Edel. "The Measure of Success in Writing." *College Composition and Communication* 43 (1978): 42–45.

DeVito, Joseph. "A Linguistic Analysis of Spoken and Written Language." *Central States Speech Association* 42 (1967): 81–85.

Dilworth, Collet, and Robert Reising. "Writing as a Moral Act: Developing a Sense of Audience." *English Journal* 67 (Nov. 1978): 74–76.

Dodge, Daniel. "English at the University of Illinois." *English in American Universities.* Ed. William Payne. Boston: Heath, 1895. 71–73.

Douglas, Loyd. "A Large Class and a Small Seminar." *College Composition and Communication* 15 (May 1964): 124–26.

Drake, Francis. "Developmental Writing." *College Composition and Communication* 1 (Dec. 1950): 3–6.

Dunning, H. D. Alpha Nu Literary Society Record Book, 1852. Michigan Historical Collections, Bentley Historical Library, University of Michigan.

Durkheim, Emile. *Sociology and Philosophy.* Trans. D. F. Pocock. London: Cohen, 1953.

Dusel, William. "How Should Student Writing Be Judged?" *English Journal* 46 (1957): 263–68.

Dyson, Anne. "Learning to Write/Learning to Do School: Emergent Writers, Interpretations of School Literacy Tasks." *Research in the Teaching of English* 18 (1984): 233–64.

———. "Second Graders Sharing Writing: The Multiple Social Realities of a Literacy Event." *Written Communication* 2 (1985): 189–215.

Eagleton, Terry. *Literary Theory: An Introduction.* Minneapolis: U of Minnesota P, 1983.

Eberhart, Wilfred. "Humanizing the Evaluation of Written Composition." *English Journal* 29 (1940): 386–93.

Ehrenberg, Randy Ann. "Clubs in English—Publish or Perish." *English Journal* 72 (Dec. 1982): 64–65.

Einhorn, L. "Oral and Written Style: An Examination of Differences." *Southern Speech Communication Journal* 43 (1978): 302–11.

Eisenstein, Elizabeth. *The Printing Press as an Agent of Change.* New York: Cambridge UP, 1979.

Elbow, Peter. "A Method for Teaching Writing." *College English* 30 (1968): 115–25.

———. "Exploring My Teaching." *College English* 32 (1971): 743–53.

———. *Writing without Teachers.* New York: Oxford, 1973.

———. Letter to the author. 26 June 1985.

Eliot, Charles. "Wherein Popular Education Has Failed." *The Forum* 14 (1892): 411–28.

Ellman, Nan. "Peer Evaluation and Peer Reading." *English Journal* 64 (Mar. 1975): 79–80.

Emerson, Caryl. "The Outer Word and Inner Speech: Bakhtin, Vygotsky and the Internalization of Language." *Critical Inquiry* 10 (1983): 245–64.

Emig, Janet. *The Composing Processes of Twelfth Graders.* Urbana: NCTE, 1971.

Erickson, John, Roland W. Holmes, and William F. Marquardt. "Preparing Student-Teachers for Composition Teaching through Writing Interaction." *College Composition and Communication* 21 (1970): 163–69.

Fadiman, Clifton, and James Howard. *Empty Pages: A Search for Writing Competence in School and Society.* Belmont, CA: Fearon, 1979.

Falk, Julia. "Language Acquisition and the Teaching and Learning of Writing." *College English* 41 (1979): 430–47.

Ferguson, Adam. *Principles of Moral and Political Science.* 1792. New York: AMS Press, 1973.

Ferster, Teresa. "An English Laboratory for Freshman." *English Journal* 26 (1937): 729–34.

Fish, Stanley. *Is There a Text in This Class: The Authority of Interpretive Communities.* Cambridge: Harvard UP, 1980.

Fisher, Martha A., and Joan Hocking. "The Writing Workshop: Boon or Bane of the Composition Classroom?" *Freshman English News* 10 (Fall 1981): 17–20.

Flanders, Ned. *Analyzing Teacher Behavior.* Reading, MA: Addison-Wesley, 1970.

Flower, Linda S., and John R. Hayes. "Problem-solving Strategies and the Writing Process." *College English* 39 (1977): 449–61.

Foucault, Michel. "What Is an Author?" *Textual Strategies: Perspectives on Structuralist Criticism.* Ed. Josue V. Harari. Ithaca: Cornell UP, 1979. 141–60.

Fox, Roy. "Treatment of Writing Apprehension and Its Effects on Composition." *Research in The Teaching of English* 14 (1980): 34–39.

Frankenburger, David. "English at the University of Wisconsin." *English in American Universities.* Ed. William Payne. Boston: Heath, 1895. 135–40.

Frantzen, Allen, and Leonard Podis. "A Modified Version of Individialized Instruction." *College Composition and Communication* 35 (1984): 234–37.

Freud, Sigmund. *Civilization and Its Discontents.* Trans. James Strachy. New York: Norton, 1968.

Fulweiler, Toby. "Showing, Not Telling at a Writing Workshop." *College English* 43 (1981): 55–63.

Gagne, Robert M., and Ernest C Smith. "A Study of the Effects of Verbalization on Problem Solving." *Journal of Experimental Psychology* 63 (1962): 12–18.

Gallagher, Helen. "An Adventure in 10B Composition." *English Journal* 26 (1937): 557–64.

Gebhardt, Richard. "Balancing Theory with Practice in the Training of Writing Teachers." *College Composition and Communication* 28 (1977): 134–40.

———. "Imagination and Discipline in the Writing Class." *English Journal* 66 (Dec. 1977): 26–32.

———. "Teamwork and Feedback: Broadening the Base of Collaborative Writing." *College English* 42 (1980): 69–74.

Gelshenen, Rosemary. "Compositions on Trial." *English Journal* 41 (1952): 431–32.

Genung, John. "English at Amherst College." *English in American Universities*. Ed. William Payne. Boston: Heath, 1895. 110–15.

George, Diana. "Working with Peer Groups in the Composition Classroom." *College Composition and Communication* 35 (1984): 320–25.

Gere, Anne Ruggles. "Written Composition: Toward a Theory of Evaluation." *College English* 42 (1980): 44–58.

———. "Public Opinion and Language." *The English Language Today*. Ed. Sidney Greenbaum. Oxford: Pergamon, 1985. 72–79.

———, ed. *Roots in the Sawdust: Writing to Learn across the Disciplines*. Urbana: NCTE, 1985.

Gere, Anne Ruggles, and Robert D. Abbott. "Talking about Writing: The Language of Writing Groups." *Research in the Teaching of English* 19 (1985a): 362–86.

Gere, Anne Ruggles, and Ralph Stevens. "The Language of Writing Groups: How Oral Response Shapes Revision." *The Acquisition of Written Language: Response and Revision*. Ed. Sarah Warshauer Freedman. Norwood, NJ: Ablex, 1985b. 85–105.

Gersten, Leon. "Getting Kids to Write Independently." *English Journal* 71 (Feb. 1982): 66–67.

Gilbert, Sandra, and Susan Gubar. *The Madwoman in the Attic*. Bloomington: Indiana UP, 1979.

Gilligan, Carol. *In A Different Voice: Psychological Theory and Women's Development*. Cambridge: Harvard UP, 1982.

Glatthorn, Alan. "Cooperate Create: Teaching Writing through Small Groups." *English Journal* 62 (1973): 1274–75.

Goodman, Nathan, ed. *A Benjamin Franklin Reader*. New York: Crowell, 1945.

Goody, Jack, ed. *Literacy in Traditional Societies*. New York: Cambridge UP, 1968.

Goor, Amos, and Ray Sommerfeld. "A Comparison of Problem-Solving Processes of Creative Students and Noncreative Students." *Journal of Educational Psychology* 67 (1975): 495–505.

Graber, Terry. "Measuring Writing Progress: An Experiment." *College English* 35 (1974): 484–85.

Graff, Harvey J. *The Literacy Myth: Literacy and Social Structure in the Nineteenth-Century City.* New York: Academic, 1979.

Graves, Donald. "An Examination of the Writing Processes of Seven Year Old Children." *Research in the Teaching of English* 9 (1975): 227–41.

———. *Writing: Teachers and Children at Work.* Exeter: Heinemann, 1983.

Green, J. R. A Comparison of Oral and Written Language: A Quantitative Analysis of the Structure and Vocabulary of the Oral and Written Language of a Group of College Students. Diss. New York U, 1958.

Greenbaum, Leonard A., and Rudolf B. Schmerl. "A Team Learning Approach to Freshman English." *College English* 29 (1967): 135–52.

Greenfield, Patricia, and Jerome Bruner. "Culture and Cognitive Growth." *Handbook of Socialization: Theory and Research.* Ed. David Goslin. New York: Rand, 1969.

Gregory, Emily. "Managing Student Writing." *English Journal* 44 (1955): 18–25.

Grissom, Loren. "Student Leadership in Evaluating Composition." *English Journal* 48 (1959): 338–39.

Hall, G. Stanley. *The Content of Children's Minds on Entering School.* New York: Kellogg, 1893.

Halliday, M. A. K. *Explorations in the Functions of Language.* London: Arnold, 1973.

Hairston, Maxine. "The Winds of Change: Thomas Kuhn and the Revolution in the Teaching of Writing." *College Composition and Communication* 33 (1982): 76–88.

Hamalion, Leo. "The Visible Voice: An Approach to Writing." *English Journal.* 59 (1970): 227–30.

Hammer, Richard. "Seven Simple Rules for Composition Instruction." *English Journal* 69 (Nov. 1980): 49–50.

Hammond, William Gardiner. *Remembrance of Amherst: An Undergraduate Diary 1846–1848.* New York: Columbia UP, 1946.

Hanneman, R. "Vision and Audition as Sensory Channels for Communication." *Quarterly Journal of Speech* 38 (1952): 162.

Hardaway, Francine. "What Students Can Do to Take the Burden off You." *College English* 36 (1974): 577–80.

Harris, Muriel. "Evaluation: The Process for Revision." *Journal of Basic Writing* 4 (1978): 82–90.

Hatfield, Wilbur. "The Project Method in Composition." *English Journal* 12 (1963): 11–23.

Hausdorff, Don. "An Experiment in Communication as Problem Solving." *College Composition and Communication* 10 (Feb. 1959): 27–32.

Havelock, Eric. *Preface to Plato*. Cambridge: Harvard UP, 1963.

Hayakawa, S. I. "Linguistic Science and the Teaching of Composition." *ETC: A Review of General Semantics* 7 (1950): 97–103.

Hawkins, Thom. *Group Inquiry Techniques for Teaching Writing*. Urbana, IL: NCTE, 1976.

———. "Intimacy and Audience: The Relation between Revision and the Social Dimension of Peer Tutoring." *College English* 42 (1980): 64–68.

Healy, Mary K. *Using Student Writing Response Groups in the Classroom*. Berkeley: Bay Area Writing Project, 1980.

Hedges, M. H. "Group Collaboration: An Experiment in Playwriting at Beloit." *English Journal* 8 (1919): 39–41.

Held, George, and Warren Rosenberg. "Student Faculty Collaboration in Teaching College Writing." *College English* 45 (1983): 817–23.

Higley, Jerry. "The New Comp." *College English* 37 (1976): 682–83.

Hilgers, Thomas. "Toward a Taxonomy of Beginning Writers' Evaluative Statements on Written Compositions." *Written Communication* 1 (1984): 365–84.

———. "On Learning the Skills of Collaborative Writing." CCC Convention. New Orleans, April 1986.

Hill, David. "The Dead Letter Office: Composition Teaching and the Writing Crisis." *College English* 39 (1978): 883–93.

Hipple, Theodore. "The Grader's Helpers—Colleagues, Peers, Scorecards." *English Journal* 61 (1981): 48–50.

Hirsch, E. D. "English and the Perils of Formalism." *American Scholar* 53 (1984): 369–79.

Hogan, Mark. "The Coaching of English." *English Journal* 69 (Oct. 1980): 22–24.

Horner, Warren. "The Economy of the Laboratory Method." *English Journal* 18 (1929): 214–21.

Horowitz, Milton, and John Newman. "Spoken and Written Expression: An Experimental Analysis." *Journal of Abnormal and Social Psychology* 68 (1964): 640–47.

Jacko, Carol. "Small-Group Triad: An Instructional Mode for the Teaching of Writing." *College Composition and Communication* 29 (1978): 290–92.

Jaech, Sharon Janson. "Going Public: A Case for Reading Aloud in the Classroom." *Rhetoric Review* 3 (Sept. 1984): 58–64.

James, Charity. *Young Lives at Stake: A Reappraisal of Secondary Schools.* London: Collins, 1968.

James, David. "Peer Teaching in the Writing Classroom." *English Journal* 70 (Nov. 1981): 48–50.

Jarabeck, Ross, and Daniel Dieterich. "Composition Evaluation: The State of the Art." *English Journal* 61 (May 1972): 690–93.

Johansson, Egil. "The History of Literacy in Sweden." *Literacy and Social Development in the West: A Reader.* Ed. Harvey Graff. Cambridge. Cambridge UP, 1981. 151–82.

John, Vera, and Leo Goldstein. "The Social Context of Language Acquisition." *Merrill Palmer Quarterly* 10 (1964): 265–75.

Johnson, Burges, and Helene Hartley. *An Outline of an Inquiry Being made at Syracuse University into the Methods, Purposes and Effectiveness of the Training of College Freshmen in Written Composition.* Syracuse: Syracuse University, 1933.

Johnson, Eric. "Avoiding Martyrdom in Teaching Writing; Some Shortcuts." *English Journal* 51 (1962): 399–402.

Judy, Stephen. "The Search for Structures in the Teaching of Composition." *English Journal* 59 (1970): 213–18.

———. "Writing for the Here and Now." *English Journal* 62 (1973): 69–79.

Kail, Harvey. "Collaborative Learning in Context: The Problem with Peer Tutoring." *College English* 45 (1983): 817–23.

Karrfalt, David. "Writing Teams: From Generating Composition to Generating Communication." *College Composition and Communication* 22 (1971): 377–78.

Kaufman, Wallace. "The Inhibited Teacher." *English Teacher* 60 (1971): 382–88.

Kelly, Lou. "Toward Competence and Creativity in an Open Class." *College English* 34 (1973): 644–60.

———."Learner-Teacher Dialogues and Writing That is Learning." *English Journal* 70 (1981): 26–29.

Kelly, Patricia, Mary Pat Hall, and Robert Small. "Composition through the Team Approach." *English Journal* 73 (Sept. 1984): 71–74.

Kinneavy, James. *A Theory of Discourse: The Aims of Discourse.* Englewood Cliffs: Prentice, 1971.

Kirby, Dan, and Tom Liner. "Revision: Yes, They Do It, Yes, You Can Teach It." *English Journal* 69 (Mar. 1980): 41–45.

Kitzhaber, Albert, "Rhetoric in American Colleges 1850–1900." Diss. U of Washington, 1953.

Kliebard, Herbert. "Education at the Turn of the Century: A Crucible for Curriculum Change." *Educational Researcher* 11 (1982): 16–24.

Kostick, Lila. "Undergraduate Workshops in Creative Writing." *College English* 13 (1952): 335–36.

Kuhn, Thomas. *The Structure of Scientific Revolutions.* Chicago: U of Chicago P, 1962.

Kuykendall, Carol. "Grammar and Composition: Myths and Realities." *English Journal* 64 (Dec. 1975): 6–7.

LaBrant, Lou. "Teaching High School Students to Write." *English Journal* 35 (1946): 123–28.

Lagana, J. R. The Development, Implementation and Evaluation of a Model for Teaching Composition Which Utilizes Individualized Learning and Peer Grouping. Diss. U of Pittsburgh, 1973.

Laird, Charlton. "Freshman English during the Flood." *College English* 18 (1956): 131–38.

Lamberg, Walter. "Self-provided and Peer-provided Feedback." *College Composition and Communication* 31 (1980): 63–69.

Langbaum, Robert. *The Poetry of Experience: The Dramatic Monologue in Modern Literary Tradition.* London: Chatto & Windus, 1957.

Lapidus-Saltz, Wendy. "The Effective Feedback Script: A Peer Response Procedure." *The Writing Instructor* 1 (1981): 19–25.

Lawson, Ray. "Composition for Seniors." *English Journal* 41 (1952): 82–85.

Leek, David. "Committee Study Improves Writing." *English Journal* 39 (1950): 455.

LeFevre, Karen Burke. *Invention as a Social Act.* Carbondale: Southern Illinois UP, 1987.

Leichter, Hope Jensen. "Families as Environments for Literacy." *Awakening to Literacy.* Ed. Hillel Goelman, Antoinette A. Oberg, and Frank Smith. Exeter: Heinemann, 1984.

Leonard, Michael. "Practice Makes Better: Notes on a Writing Program." *English Journal* 65 (Sept. 1976): 59–63.

Leonard, Sterling. "Two Types of Criticism for Composition Work." *English Journal* 5 (1916): 508–9.

———. *English Composition as a Social Problem.* Boston: Houghton, 1917.

Liftig, Robert. "After Basics." *English Journal* 71 (Oct. 1982): 47–50.

Lindsay, Barbara. "The Class That Does Not Meet." *College Composition and Communication* 17 (Dec. 1966): 258–60.

Literary Adelphi Record Book. Michigan Historical Collections, Bentley Historical Library, University of Michigan.

Livingston, Lorraine. "An Experiment in Correction and Revision." *College English* 18 (1956): 169–70.

Lord, Mrs. A. A. "The Social Club." *New England Journal of Education* 11 (1880): 178–86.

Lunsford, Andrea, and Lisa Ede. "Singular Texts/Plural Authors." Unpublished ms.

Lyle, Guy R. "College Literary Societies in the Fifties." *Library Quarterly* 4 (1934): 487–93.

Lynch, Denise. "Easing the Process: A Strategy for Evaluating Compositions." *College Composition and Communication* 33 (1982): 310–14.

Lyons, Bill. "The PQP Method of Responding to Writing." *English Journal* 70 (Mar. 1981): 42–43.

McGann, Jerome J. *A Critique of Modern Textual Criticism.* Chicago: U of Chicago P, 1983.

McKee, Mabel. "Three Examples of Motivation." *English Journal* 9 (1920): 457–62.

MacLean, George. "English at the University of Minnesota." *English in American Universities.* Ed. William Payne. Boston: Heath, 1895. 155–62.

MacLean, Marion. "Voices Within: An Audience Speaks." *English Journal* 72 (Nov. 1983): 62–66.

McNamara, John. "Teaching the Process of Writing." *College English* 34 (1973): 661–65.

Macrorie, Ken. "Words in the Way." *English Journal* 40 (1951): 382–85.

———. *Writing to Be Read.* Rochelle, NJ: Hayden, 1968. [a]

———. "To Be Read." *English Journal* 57 (1968): 686–92. [b]

———. "Writing's Dying." *College Composition and Communication* 11 (Dec. 1960): 206–10.

———. *Writing to Be Read*. 2nd ed. Rochelle, NJ: Hayden, 1976.

———. *Writing to Be Read*. 3rd ed. Upper Montclair, NJ: Boynton/Cook, 1984.

———. *Uptaught*. Rochelle, NJ: Hayden, 1970.

Maheu, R. World Congress of Ministers of Education on the Eradication of Illiteracy. Speech and Messages, UNESCO. Teheran, 1966. Quoted in *Modes of Thought*. Ed. Robin Horton and Ruth Finnegan. London: Faber, 1973.

Maimon, Elaine P. "Talking to Strangers." *College Composition and Communication* 30 (1979): 364–69.

Maize, Ray. "The Partner Method of Review at the Air Command and Staff School." *College English* 12 (1951): 396–99.

———. "A Writing Laboratory for Retarded Students." *College English* 16 (1954): 44–48.

Mann, M. "The Quantitative Differentiation of Samples of Written Language." *Psychological Monographs* 56 (1944): 41–74.

Marcus, Harriet. "The Writing Center: Peer Tutoring in a Supportive Setting." *English Journal* 73 (Sept. 1984): 66–67.

Marx, Karl. *Economic and Philosophical Manuscripts of 1844*. Trans. Thomas Martin Millegan. New York: International, 1964.

Mason, Edwin. *Collaborative Learning*. London: Ward Lock, 1970.

Mason, Marybeth. "A Vacation That Sustained Me for Three Years." *English Journal* 70 (Apr. 1981): 43–44.

Maxwell, William. "An Experiment in Correcting Compositions." *Educational Review* 7 (1894): 240–46.

Mead, David. *Yankee Eloquence in the Middle West: The Ohio Lyceum 1850–1870*. East Lansing: Michigan State College Press, 1951.

Megna, Jerome. "Teaching Writing Skills through Peer Evaluation." *The English Record* 2 (1976): 98–106.

Mersand, Joseph. "What Has Happened to Written Composition?" *English Journal* 50 (1961): 231–37.

Messelaar, Dirk. "The Use of Peer Rating Scales in Teaching Writing." *The English Record* 27 (Winter 1976): 17–19.

Michaels, Sarah. "Sharing Time: Children's Narrative Styles and Differential Access to Literacy." *Language and Society* 10 (1981): 423–42.

Mishler, Elliot. "Implications of Teacher Strategies for Language and Cognition: Observations in First Grade Classrooms." *Functions of Language in the Classroom*. Ed. Courtney Cazden, Vera John, and Dell Hymes. New York: Teachers College Press, 1972. 267–98.

Moffett, James. *Teaching the Universe of Discourse*. Boston: Houghton Mifflin, 1968.

Monday Club. Records. Box 1. Archive Division, Suzallo Library, University of Washington.

Moore, Joseph. "A Writing Week." *English Journal* 67 (Nov. 1978): 39–41.

Morley, Dave, and Ken Worpole, eds. *The Republic of Letters: Working Class Writing and Local Publishing*. London: Comedia, 1982.

Morris, Robert. "The Theme-of-the-Week-Club." *English Journal* 18 (1929): 28–31.

Munz, Martin. "Using the Projector in Written Composition." *English Journal* 28 (1939): 130–31.

Murray, Donald. *A Writer Teaches Writing*. Boston: Houghton Mifflin, 1968.

———. "Finding Your Own Voice: Teaching Composition in an Age of Dissent." *College Composition and Communication* 20 (1969): 118–23.

———. "Internal Revision: A Process of Discovery." *Research on Composing*. Ed. Charles Cooper and Lee Odell. Urbana: NCTE, 1978.

. Letter to the author. 26 September 1984.

———. *A Writer Teaches Writing*. 2nd ed. Boston: Houghton, 1985.

Myers, Miles. "What Kind of People Talk That Way?" *English Journal* 70 (Nov. 1981): 24–29.

NCTE Commission on Composition. "Teaching Composition: A Position Statement." *College English* 46 (1984): 612–14.

National Writing Project. *Evaluation Portfolio*. Berkeley: U of California, 1984.

Newell, Allen, and Herbert A. Simon. *Human Problem Solving*. Englewood Cliffs: Prentice-Hall, 1972.

Newkirk, Thomas. "Direction and Misdirection in Peer Response." *College Composition and Communication* 35 (1984): 301–11. [a]

———. "How Students Read Student Papers." *Written Communication* 1 (1984): 283–305. [b]

Newland, Fay. "English Laboratory." *English Journal* 34 (1945): 379–83.

Nineteenth Century Literary Club. Yearbook, 1903. Northwest Collection. Suzallo Library, University of Washington.

North, Stephen. "The Idea of a Writing Center." *College English* 46 (1984): 433–46.

Noyes, Ernest. "Class Criticism as a Means of Teaching English Composition." *School Review* 13 (1905): 696–701.

Nye, Russell. *Society and Culture in America 1830–1860.* New York: Harper, 1974.

Nystrand, Martin. "Learning to Write by Talking about Writing: A Summary of Intensive Peer Review in Expository Writing Instruction at the University of Wisconsin-Madison." *The Structure of Written Communication.* Ed. Martin Nystrand. New York: Academic, forthcoming.

O'Donnell, Angela, Donald Danserau, Thomas Rocklin, Judity Lambiotte, Velma Hytherker, and Celia Larson. "Cooperative Writing: Direct Effects and Transfer. " *Written Communication* 2 (1985): 307–15.

Olson, David. "From Utterance to Text: The Bias of Language in Speech and Writing." *Harvard Educational Review* 47 (1977): 257–81.

Ong, Walter. *Ramus, Method and the Decay of Dialogue.* Cambridge: Harvard UP, 1958.

Orchard, Hugh. *Fifty Years of Chautauqua.* Cedar Rapids: Torch, 1923.

Oxenham, John. *Literacy: Writing, Reading and Social Organisation.* London: Routledge, 1980.

Parker, Richard Green. *Aids to English Composition.* New York: Harper, 1870.

Pattison, Robert. *On Literacy.* New York: Oxford UP, 1982.

Paul, Bernice. "Group Participation in Theme-Writing." *English Journal* 39 (1950): 455.

Peckham, Irvin "Peer Evaluation." *English Journal* 67 (Oct. 1978): 61–63.

———. "A Teacher Learning to Write." *English Journal* 69 (Nov. 1980): 43–51.

Perl, Sondra. "The Composing Processes of Unskilled College Writers." *Research in the Teaching of English* 13 (1979): 317–36.

Peterson, Bruce T. "Writing about Responses: A Unified Model of Reading, Interpretation, and Composition." *College English* 44 (1982): 459–68.

Pfister, Fred R., and Joanne F. Petrik. "A Heuristic Model for Creating a Writer's Audience." *College Composition and Communication* 31 (1980): 213–20.

Phelps, Louise Wetherbee. "The Dance of Discourse: A Dynamic Relativistic View of Structure." *Pretext* 3 (1982): 51–83.

Piaget, Jean. *The Construction of Reality in the Child.* New York: Basic, 1954.

———. *Language and Thought of a Child.* New York: Basic, 1954.

Podis, Leonard. "Training Peer Tutors for the Writing Lab." *College Composition and Communication* 31 (1980): 70–75.

Portnoy, S. "A Comparison of Oral and Written Verbal Behavior." *Studies in Verbal Behavior: An Empirical Approach.* Ed. K Salzinger and R. S. Feldman. New York: Pergamon, 1973.

Potter, David, *Debating in the Colonial Chartered Colleges: An Historical Survey 1642–1900.* New York: Teachers College Press, 1944.

Potts, Ralph. Minutes of Seattle Writers' Club 1909–1916. Ralph Potts Papers, Box 3. Archive Division, Suzallo Library, University of Washington.

Prince, Ellen. "Toward a Taxonomy of Given-New Information." *Radical Pragmatics.* Ed. Peter Cole. New York: Academic, 1981.

Pumphrey, Jean. "Teaching English Composition as a Creative Art." *College English* 34 (1973): 666–73.

Putz, Joan. "When the Teacher Stops Teaching: An Experiment with Freshman English." *College English* 32 (1970): 50–57.

Quadrangle Society Record Book. Michigan Historical Collections, Bentley Historical Library, University of Michigan

Quarante Club. 1910–1980. Box 1. Archive Division, Suzallo Library, University of Washington.

Queen Ann Fortnightly. Yearbook (1906). Northwest Collection, Suzallo Library, University of Washington.

Reither, James. "Writing and Knowing: Toward Redefining the Writing Process." *College English* 47 (1985): 620–28.

Report of Workshop. "From Reading to Writing." *College Composition and Communication* 5 (Oct. 1954): 126–30.

———. "Unprecedentedly Large Classes: Exploratory Solutions." *College Composition and Communication* 7 (Oct. 1956): 167–69.

Rice, Joseph M. *The Public School System of the United States.* New York: Century, 1893.

———. *Scientific Management in Education.* New York: Hinds, 1913.

Rizzo, Betty. "Peer Teaching in English." *College Composition and Communication* 26 (1975): 394–96.

Robbins, Katharine. "The Work of the American Speech Committee of the Chicago Women's Club and Notes upon its School Survey." *English Journal* 7 (1918): 163–76.

Roberts, H. D. "Building the Creative Audience." *English Journal* 19 (1930): 751–52.

Robinson, A. T. "The Question of Text-Books in Composition." *Science* 37 (1913): 60–63.

Rorty, Richard. *Philosophy and the Mirror of Nature.* Princeton: Princeton UP, 1979.

Rothman, Donald. "Tutoring in Writing: Our Literacy Problem." *College English* 39 (1977): 484–90.

Rouse, John. "Scenes from the Writing Workshop." *College English* 47 (1985): 217–36.

Rubin, Donnalee. "Evaluating Freshman Writers: What Do Students Really Learn?" *College English* 45 (1983): 373–79.

Salerno, Grayce Faley. "An English Laboratory in Action." *English Journal* 52 (1963): 37–41.

Saussure, Ferdinand de. *Course in General Linguistics.* Ed. Charles Bally and Albert Sechehaye. Trans. Wade Baskin. New York: The Philosophical Library, 1959.

Schelling, Felix. "English at the University of Pennsylvania." *English in American Universities.* Ed. William Payne. Boston: Heath, 1895. 130–34.

Schuster, Charles. "The Un-Assignment: Writing Groups for Advanced Expository Writers." *Freshman English News* 13 (Winter 1984): 433–46.

Schwarz, Judith. *Radical Feminists of Heterodoxy: Greenwich Village 1912–1940.* Lebanon, NH: New Victoria, 1982.

Scott, Fred Newton. "English Composition as a Mode of Behavior." *English Journal* 11 (1922): 463–73.

Scott, Fred Newton, and Joseph V. Denney. *Elementary English Composition.* Norwood: Norwood P, 1900.

Scribner, Sylvia, and Michael Cole. *The Psychology of Literacy.* Cambridge: Harvard UP, 1981.

Sears, Connie. "A Letter Home from the Oklahoma Writing Project." *English Journal* 70 (Apr. 1981): 45.

Seattle Branch, National League of American Penwomen. Minutes. Boxes 3 and 4. Archive Division, Suzallo Library, University of Washington.

Seattle Women's Century Club. Record Book. Northwest Collection. Suzallo Library, University of Washington.

Shaughnessy, Mina. *Errors and Expectations.* New York: Oxford UP, 1977.

Shuman, R. Baird. "What about Revision?" *English Journal* 64 (Dec. 1975): 41–43.

Sinclair, J., and R. M. Coulthard. *Toward an Analysis of Discourse: The English Used by Teachers and Pupils.* Oxford: Oxford UP, 1975.

Smith, F., and G. A. Miller. *The Genesis of Language.* Cambridge: MIT Press, 1966.

Smith, R. R. "Increasing Satisfactory Production in Composition." *English Journal* 14 (1925): 466–71.

Smith, Shirley. "Fred Newton Scott as a Teacher." *Michigan Alumnus* 4 (Feb. 1933): 279–80.

Snipes, Wilson Currin. "An Inquiry: Peer Group Teaching in Freshman Writing." *College Composition and Communication* 22 (1971): 169–74.

———. "Oral Composing as an Approach to Writing." *College Composition and Communication* 24 (1973): 200–205.

Sochatoff, A. F. "One Hundred Years." *The First One Hundred Years of the Zelosophic Literary Society.* Ed. Thomas Birch. Philadelphia: U of Pennsylvania, 1929.

Soltow, Lee and Edward Stevens. *The Rise of Literacy and the Common School in the United States: A Socioeconomic Analysis to 1870.* Chicago: U of Chicago P, 1981.

Sommers, Nancy. "Revision Strategies of Student Writers and Experienced Adult Writers." *College Composition and Communication* 31 (1980): 378–88.

Sorenson, Frederick. "New Methods in Freshman English." *College English* 14 (1952): 161–63.

Stade, George. "Hydrands into Elephants: The Theory and Practice of College Composition." *College English* 31 (1969): 143–54.

Stallard, Charles. "An Analysis of the Writing Behavior of Good Student Writers." *Research in the Teaching of English* 8 (1974): 206–18.

Stern, D. N. "Mother and Infant at Play: The Dyadic Interaction Involving Facial, Social and Gaze Behaviors." *The Effect of the Infant on its Caregiver.* Ed. M. Lewis and L. A. Rosenblum. New York: Wiley, 1974.

Sternberg, Robert J. "What Should Intelligence Tests Test? Implications of a Triarchic Theory of Intelligence for Intelligence Testing." *Educational Researcher* 13 (1984): 5–15.

———. *Beyond IQ: A Triarchic Theory of Human Intelligence.* New York: Cambridge UP, 1985.

Steward, Joyce. "To Like to Have Written: Learning the Laboratory Way." *ADE Bulletin* 6 (Sept. 1975): 32–40.

Stewart, Donald. "The Most Important Exercise of All: Rewriting in Class." *College Composition and Communication* 18 (Feb. 1967): 56–58.

———. "Some Facts Worth Knowing about the Origins of Freshman Composition." *CEA Critic* 44 (1982): 2–11.

Stock, Brian. *The Implications of Literacy. Written Language and Models of Interpretation in the Eleventh and Twelfth Centuries.* Princeton: Princeton UP, 1983.

Strang, Steven. "Process and Product: The Author-Led Workshop." *College Composition and Communication* 35 (1984): 327–33.

Strawson, P. F. *Logico-Linguistic Papers.* London: Methuen, 1971.

Street, Brian. *Literacy in Theory and Practice.* Cambridge: Cambridge UP, 1984.

Strout, Beverly. "Writing Workshop: What Is It?" *English Journal* 59 (1970): 1128–30.

Tannen, Deborah. "Relative Focus on Interpersonal Involvement in Oral and Written Discourse." *Literacy, Language and Learning: The Nature and Consequences of Reading and Writing.* Ed. David Olson, Nancy Torrance, and Angela Hildgard. New York: Cambridge UP, 1985. 124–47.

Thie, Thomas. "Testing the Efficiency of the Group Method." *English Journal* 14 (1925): 134–37.

Thimmesch, Nick. *Aliteracy: People Who Can Read But Won't.* Washington D.C.: American Enterprise Institute for Public Policy Research, 1984.

Thompson, C. J. "A Study of the Socialized versus the Academic Method of Teaching Written Composition." *School Review* 27 (1919): 110–33.

Thurber, Samuel. "English Literature in Girls' Education." *The School Review* 11 (1894): 321–36.

———. "Five Axioms of Composition Teaching." *School Review* 5 (1897): 7–17.

Thwing, Charles. *A History of Higher Education in America.* New York: Appleton, 1906.

Tomlinson, Barbara. "Cooking, Mining, Gardening, Hunting: Metaphorical Stories Writers Tell about Their Writing Processes." *Metaphor and Symbolic Activity*, forthcoming.

Toulmin, Stephen. "The Inwardness of Mental Life." *Critical Inquiry* 6 (1979): 1–16.

Tovatt, Anthony and Ebert L. Miller. "The Sound of Writing." *Research in the Teaching of English* 1 (1967): 56–58.

Tressler, Jacob. "The Efficiency of Student Correction of Compositions." *English Journal* 1 (1912): 405–11.

Trevarthen, C., and P. Hubley. "Secondary Intersubjectivity: Confidence, Confiding, and Acts of Meaning in the First Year." *Action, Gesture and Symbol: The Emergence of Language*. Ed. A. J. Lock. London: Academic Press, 1978.

Trimble, John. *Writing with Style*. Englewood Cliffs: Prentice, 1975.

Trimbur, John. "Beyond Cognition: The Rhetoric of Inner Speech." CCC Convention. New York, Mar. 1984.

———. "Collaborative Learning and Teaching Writing." *Perspectives on Research and Scholarship in Composition*. Ed. Ben W. McClelland and Timothy R. Donovan. New York: MLA, 1985. 87–109.

Tsujimato, James. "Revisioning the Whole." *English Journal* 73 (Sept. 1984): 53–55.

Vachek, J. *Written Language: General Problems and Problems of English*. The Hague: Mouton, 1973.

Valentine, Robert G. "On Criticism of Themes by Students." *The Technology Review* 4 (1902): 459–78.

Villanueva, Victor. The Conscious Consideration of Sound in the Composing Processes of Basic and Traditional College Freshmen. Diss. U of Washington, 1988.

Vincent, John. *The Chautauqua Movement*. New York: Books for Libraries, 1885.

Vygotsky, Lev. *Thought and Language*. Trans. Eugenia Hanfmann and Gertrude Vakar. Cambridge: MIT, 1962.

———. *Mind in Society: The Development of Higher Psychological Processes*. Ed. Michael Cole et al. Cambridge: Harvard UP, 1978.

Wagner, Eileen. "How to Avoid Grading Compositions." *English Journal* 64 (1975): 2–8.

Walker, Amasa. "An Address Delivered before the Young Men of Boston, Associated for Moral and Intellectual Improvement, on the Fifty-Seventh Anniversary of American Independence." *The Christian Examiner* 15 (1833): 120–33.

Walker, Francis. "The Laboratory System in English." *English Journal* 6 (1917): 445–53.

Walsh, E. Michael. "Teaching the Letter of Application." *College English* 39 (1977): 484–90.

Ward, Bertha Evans. "A Writing Group and the School Magazine." *English Journal* 22 (1933): 289–96.

Ward, Lester Frank. *Dynamic Sociology.* New York: Appleton, 1883.

———. *Psychic Factors of Civilization.* Boston: Ginn, 1893.

Watt, Homer A. "The Philosophy of Real Composition." *English Journal* 7 (1918): 153–62.

Wayne, R. The Effects of Peer Grading/Editing on the Grammar-Usage and Theme Composition Ability of College Freshmen. Diss. U of Oklahoma, 1973.

Wednesday P. M. Club. Yearbook (1902). Northwest Collection. Suzallo Library, University of Washington.

Welch, Jack. "On the Importance of Cohesiveness in Writing Classes." *College Composition and Communication* 24 (1973): 200–205.

Welter, Barbara. "The Cult of True Womanhood: 1820–1860." *American Quarterly* 18 (1966): 151–74.

Wertsch, James V. *Vygotsky and the Social Formation of Mind.* Cambridge: Harvard UP, 1985.

Wheeler, Paul Mowbray. "Advanced English Composition." *English Journal* 19 (1930): 557–66.

White, John O. "Students Learn by Doing Holistic Scoring." *English Journal* 71 (Nov. 1982): 50–51.

Wiener, Harvey. "Collaborative Learning in the Classroom: A Guide to Evaluation." *College English* 48 (1986): 52–61.

Wilbers, Stephen. *The Iowa Writers' Workshop: Origins, Emergence, and Growth.* Iowa City: U of Iowa P, 1981.

Wilcox, Thomas. "The Varieties of Freshman English." *College English* 33 (1972): 686–701.

Williams, Raymond. *Writing in Society.* London: Verso, 1983.

Wixon, Vincent, and Pat Stone. "Getting It Out, Getting It Down: Adapting Zoellner's Talk-Write." *English Journal* 66 (Sept. 1977): 70–73.

Wolf, H. R. "Composition and Group Dymanics: The Paradox of Freedom." *College English* 30 (1969): 441–44.

Women's Tuesday Club. Yearbook, 1904. Northwest Collection, Suzallo Library, University of Washington.

Wood, Ann. "The 'Scribbling' Women and Fanny Fern: Why Women Wrote." *American Quarterly* 23 (1971): 3–24.

Woodmansee, Martha. "The Genius and the Copyright: Economic and Legal Conditions of the Emergence of the 'Author.'" *Eighteenth Century Studies* 17 (1984): 425–48.

Woods, William. "The Reform Tradition in Nineteenth-Century Composition Teaching." *Written Composition* 2 (1985): 377–90.

Woody, Thomas. *A History of Women's Education in the United States.* New York: Science, 1929.

Woolbert, C. "Speaking and Writing: A Study of Difference." *Quarterly Journal of Speech Education* 8 (1922): 277–78.

Wozniak, John Michael. *English Composition in Eastern Colleges, 1850–1940.* Washington, D.C.: University Press, 1978.

Wright, J. G. "The First Year English in the High School." *The School Review* 1 (1892): 15–23.

Ylvisaker, Miriam. "Writing Workshop: A Fantasy at Reality Level." *English Journal* 69 (Dec. 1980): 70–75.

Young, Edward. "Conjectures on Original Composition." *English Critical Essays Sixteenth, Seventeenth and Eighteenth Centuries.* Ed. Edmund Jones. New York: Oxford, 1947.

Ziegler, Carl. "Laboratory Method in English Teaching." *English Journal* 8 (1919): 143–53.

Zoellner, Robert. "Talk-Write. A Behavioral Pedagogy for Composition." *College English* 30 (1969): 267–320.

Anne Ruggles Gere received her Ph.D. from the University of Michigan and is currently Associate Professor of English at the University of Washington, where she specializes in rhetoric and composition. Her articles have appeared in *College English, College Composition and Communication, Research in the Teaching of English,* and *English Journal.* She is author of *Roots in the Sawdust: Writing to Learn across the Disciplines* and *Writing and Learning* and is coauthor, with Eugene Smith, of *Language, Attitudes and Change.*